DATE DUE

FEB 2 7 2001			

Demco

THE SAVAGE VIEW

Charles Savage, Pioneer Mormon Photographer

C.R.SAVAGE.PHOTO.

LAKE FRONT. SALTAIR BEACH. GT. SALT LAKE

THE SAVAGE VIEW

Charles Savage, Pioneer Mormon Photographer

Bradley W. Richards, M.D.

CARL MAUTZ PUBLISHING

1995

Copyright © 1995 by Carl Mautz Publishing
Text copyright © 1995 by Bradley W. Richards, M.D.
All rights reserved in all countries.

Designed by Richard D. Moore
Edited by Jeanne Chapman
Type composed in Adobe Garamond
Printed and bound in Korea by Dai Nippon Printing

Cover: *Meeting of Locomotives at Promontory, 1869.* From a stereoview by Charles Savage.
Frontispiece: *Lake Front, Saltair Beach.* Photograph by Charles Savage. Collection of L.D.S. Church Archives.
Back cover: *Royal Arch Yucca of the Mojave Desert.* Photograph by Charles Savage. Collection of L.D.S. Church Archives.

FIRST EDITION
1 3 5 7 9 10 8 6 4 2

Library of Congress Catalog No. 94-77983

LIBRARY OF CONGRESS CATALOGING-IN-PUBLICATION DATA
   Richards, Bradley W.
     The Savage view: Charles Savage, pioneer Mormon photographer/by Bradley W. Richards.
   p. cm.
   Includes bibliographical references (p.) and index.
   ISBN 0-9621940-5-0.—ISBN 0-9621940-6-9 (pbk.)

     1. Savage, C. R. (Charles Roscoe), 1832-1909. 2. Photographers—West (U.S.)—Biography. 3. Photography—West
(U.S.)—History. 4. Mormons—West (U.S.)—Biography. I. Title

   TR140.S38A3 1995   770'.92
                                         QBI95-980

CARL MAUTZ PUBLISHING   Telephone (916) 478-1610
229 Commercial Street, No. 522   Facsimile (916) 478-0466
Nevada City, California 95959   E-Mail: FolkImage@aol.com

CONTENTS

To my father, Winn L. Richards, M.D., the finest man I have ever known,
and to my mother, Joyce W. Richards, who taught me to cherish all that is good
and beautiful in this world.

MY INTEREST in Charles Savage began in 1989, when I first saw several of his magnificent photographs of nineteenth-century Utah. Having been raised in Utah, and having an interest in both history and photography, I was enchanted by these beautiful images. I resolved to learn more about this photographer. As I began my research, I found that some information was readily available, but much of it was conflicting or incomplete. (I later learned that Savage's life was far better recorded than were most nineteenth-century photographers, since he left diaries, scrapbooks, newspaper advertisements, and many other references.) The desire to learn more about Savage's life and work quickly expanded to become a near obsession, and eventually it lead to the writing of this book.

As I searched for material on Charles Savage, I discovered that each new source of information opened up several new sources, and at least as many new questions about his life. Although I have striven to be as thorough as possible, I have found that each time I explored a new lead, I invariably encountered another researcher with more information, resulting in yet another revision of my text. Eventually, I accepted the advice of several colleagues, who told me that research was a never-ending cycle, and that I should go ahead, publish the book, and wait for future developments to clarify some of the details. This book, therefore, is intended not as the definitive source of information on Charles Savage, but rather as a benchmark for further research. I sincerely hope that future students and researchers will be kind enough to reveal my errors and allow me to assist in their research.

Throughout my research on Savage and other Western scenic photographers, I have been amazed and gratified by the willingness of professional researchers, collectors, and archivists to help an amateur like myself. Almost every person I contacted during my research has been helpful, far beyond the bounds of simple courtesy. Some of these people deserve special mention.

I am indebted, as are most photographic historians, for the groundwork laid by Nelson Wadsworth. His tireless work over the last thirty years has resulted in the preservation of many priceless photographic collections in university archives, including the Savage journals and scrapbook at the Brigham Young University Archives. I am especially grateful to him for his assistance in obtaining photographs for this book, and for his early writings on Savage, which form a basis for this biography.

I am also grateful to Sally Sharp Lloyd, Louise Clark Benion, and Harrison Brothers, all descendants of Savage, who opened their homes to me and helped to find important information. Other descendants of Savage have also contacted me, each with further information to share. Barry Swackhamer, a photographic collector and researcher, located many crucial and rare images, and put me in contact with many other researchers. Bill Slaughter and Randall Dixon at the Church of Jesus Christ of Latter-day Saints History Department Archives were especially helpful, not only in finding details about Savage photographs, but for their boundless enthusiasm and encouragement, which helped me through discouraging moments. I appreciate as well researchers in other areas for their assistance in clarifying the often complex relationships between Savage and other photographers. Jim Deardon and Susan Williams provided information on Andrew J. Russell; Glen Willumsen on Alfred Hart; and Jennifer Lund on her great-grandfather, Charles Carter. I am also indebted to Gloria Palmer, reference librarian at the Davis County Library, for aid in locating many obscure references on Savage, and Drew Ross of the University of Utah Archives for help in editing.

Finally, great appreciation is due my wife Cristina, and my children, Rebecca, Brian, David, and Meghan, from whom most of the time used in writing this biography was taken, and who supported me in my obsession with a long-dead photographer. Without their support and love, I could not have finished this book.

INTRODUCTION

By William W. Slaughter

CHARLES Roscoe Savage (1832-1909) was a Mormon, a pioneer, and a photographer. Indeed, he was a "pioneer photographer" who learned the art of photography in its infancy and continually kept on the forefront of its rapidly changing technology.

Savage was not simply an early photographer—he was an excellent photographer. Gaining prominence early in his career, he was considered a "name" photographer who was respected and sought out by his peers throughout the nation. He counted the finest photographers in the West among his friends, including Carleton P. Watkins, A. J. Russell, Timothy O'Sullivan, and William Henry Jackson among many others. In addition, numerous Utah residents, government officials, and Mormon Church leaders posed before Savage's camera.

While adept at portraiture, he was perhaps at his best when photographing the landscape of Utah, the Rocky Mountain area, and the West. He also documented the growth and development of Salt Lake City and its vicinity. Savage's pursuit of landscape photography did not evolve in a vacuum. In the United States, the period from about 1860 to 1885 was a "golden age" of intense outdoor photographic endeavor that grew out of and coincided with a heightened appreciation of nature in literature and painting. Savage's friendships with artist George Ottinger and artist/writer Alfred Lambourne heightened his artistic awareness of the grandeur of nature, giving him a finer eye for perspective while photographing the landscape.

There also was the practical side to C. R. Savage's outdoor photography. Until the advent of simple portable cameras (the first of which was marketed in 1883, the public was dependent upon professional photographers for landscape views and portraits. Early on, Savage realized that for his business to be successful, he would have to travel extensively over much of the western United States. A boon to his business was the willingness of the Union Pacific and the Denver and Rio Grande railroad companies to supply Savage with free passes and an occasional private railroad car for his photographic expeditions. Of course, the railroad companies used these western scenes to entice eastern tourists to visit the West via their railroads.

Savage soon learned that selling photographs was a profitable business, particularly if you were willing to stay on top of the latest trends and learn the newest photographic technology. Unlike many of his fellow photographers, Savage, was able to balance the artistic and the "practical" business side of a photographic vocation. His professional career spanned fifty years, during which time he won first prize for his photographs at world expositions in Chicago, St. Louis, San Francisco and Portland.

In addition to being an accomplished photographer, Savage was a member of the Salt Lake Tabernacle Choir, a captain in the Utah Nauvoo Legion, an ecclesiastical leader in the Salt Lake Stake, and a co-founder of Utah's "Old Folks Days." He delivered popular illustrated lectures on the West, contributed articles to local and national publications, and supported the arts in Utah. His was a life filled with doing and accomplishment.

Dr. Bradley Richards has spent five years

studying the life and photography of Charles R. Savage. While articles and chapters of books have been written about aspects of Savage's life, this is the first book-length biography of Savage. Surely his is a life worth examining. Dr. Richards is to be commended for re-establishing the prominence of the work and life of this important western photographer.

William W. Slaughter
Chief Photo-Archivist
Historical Department
Church of Jesus Christ of Latter-day Saints

CHAPTER I

A Saint from Southampton

JOHN Savage, of Southampton, Hampshire, England, worked as a gardener on an old English estate. He was a quiet man of easy temperament, but unfortunately was quite unsuccessful in financial matters. He and his wife, Ann Rogers, lived in a poor area of Southampton. Very little is known about the immediate forebears of John and Ann Savage other than a few names and a coat-of-arms.[1] Into this quiet family, at four o'clock in the afternoon on August 16, 1832, was born their first son, Charles Roscoe Savage. Two other sons, George and James, as well as a daughter, Ann, were later added to this humble household.

As a child of three or four years, Charles had a narrow escape from death when a burning chip of wood from the fireplace ignited his clothing. He was badly burned, but stated that "a neighbor by the name of Nutbeam [had] the presence of mind to keep the burnt portion of my body well oiled by which my body was kept from being marked or disfigured with the exception of a mark on the right and left cheeks."[2] Through the kindness of a woman named Mrs. Bond, he attended St. Mary's National School. He played truant with several other boys for a week, however, and when punished by "receiving the burch" he left school, thus ending his formal education after only nine months.

At this time in England a large reward was offered for a blue dahlia, and the elder Savage spent most of his spare time trying to produce one, neglecting his family's welfare. None of the children were able to obtain any further education, and Charles was put out to work at a very young age to help support the family. He had a number of jobs in his youth, but work was hard to find in a crowded country such as England. He found the world cold and heartless, and would later reflect that he could remember no one during his youth who ever helped him or was interested in his welfare. Despite the harshness of his early years, young Savage developed a kind and jovial nature. Some of his boyhood acquaintances remained his close friends for life. One of his jobs as a child was that of selling salt door-to-door in Southampton, a tedious task yielding only meager profits. He peddled salt in the neighborhood of a coach-making shop operated by a Henry Puzey, who let the boy turn the grindstone where he sharpened his tools. In return for this Charles was paid a shilling, a welcome addition to his salt-seller's wages. Years later, when Henry and Charles had both moved to the United States, they were still friends, and Savage spoke at Puzey's funeral in 1896.[3]

These hard times taught Charles that he could depend only on himself for his welfare. Although he later became a successful businessman, and was generous almost to a fault, he was always frugal, and kept strict accounts of each penny earned and spent. He later said that through all of these hardships he felt constantly "buoyed up" by a hopeful feeling that seemed to point toward a better future. He also developed an interest in religion during these early years. He later wrote:

FIGURE 2. (OPPOSITE)
View of Southampton, Hampshire, England, c. 1870. Original print in Savage Book of Remembrance.

FIGURE 3.
Coat-of-arms of the Savage family of England and Scotland. Original print in Savage Book of Remembrance.

FIGURE 4.
T. B. H. Stenhouse, the missionary who helped convert young Charles Savage to the Mormon Church, as he appeared in later life. Photograph from L.D.S. Church Archives.

In my life I had been miraculously preserved from various dangers which I now know to have been by the power of God. Many times have want and hunger stared us all in the face, many have been the schemes I was up to to obtain a shilling or two, but through it all the Lord preserved me.

By the age of thirteen or fourteen, somewhat bitter and disillusioned with the world, Savage began investigating the local churches in Southampton. He had received little religious instruction from his parents, and he felt compelled to learn more. Along with a friend, Frederick Rogers, he "went from Church to Chapel, seeking something, we knew not what." One night, at age sixteen, he spotted an announcement stating that "an Elder of the Church of Jesus Christ was come to proclaim the coming of an angel."

I communicated my discovery to Fred, who agreed with me to hear this gentleman, namely T. B. H. Stenhouse, we accordingly went on a Sunday evening in February 1848 to a room in Albion Place at the top of the house, but when we arrived at the room there stood the individual who was to make his debut before a Southampton audience, but anticipating we were come to enjoy a lark at his expense he told us there was no fire there, and held out no inducement for us to go up, but I was not to be baffled out of my object, so I went upstairs followed by Fred . . .

. . . At length the time arrived for the meeting to commence, then again did my feelings roam in the realm of fancy to imagine what I should hear, but alas! how differ-

ent to my anticipations, although not capable of fairly judging a subject of a religious character, still I could see that there was truth in what was advanced, but the most strange features that characterized my visit there was: the fact of my having no desire to roam further in the religious hemisphere. Here my search ended. I felt no desire to go further, with the little knowledge I then possessed I could see that the principles which were from time to time advocated in that place were the most tangible of any religious notions I had entertained. After I had heard the first lecture on Mormonism my mind began to expand . . . I felt that my lot sooner or later must be cast among this people.

"This people," with whom Savage was to spend the rest of his life, were the Mormons, or members of the Church of Jesus Christ of Latter-day Saints. The history of the L.D.S. Church, as it is also known, began in western New York with a young man named Joseph Smith. In 1820, when he was fourteen years old, Joseph Smith had a vision in which God and His Son, Jesus Christ, appeared to him. Seven years later, Joseph Smith was given an ancient record, inscribed upon plates of gold, that was hidden in a hillside near his home. These plates were translated by Smith through the power of God, and are a record of God's dealings with the former inhabitants of the American continent the ancestors of the American Indians. This record, called the Book of Mormon after the ancient prophet who compiled the record, became part of the scriptures used by members of the L.D.S. Church, along with the Bible. Members of the church were called "Mormons" after the title of this book. This nickname was originally an epithet used by enemies of the young religion, but it soon became a common name for members of the Church of Jesus Christ of Latter-day Saints, and was used by members and non-members alike. Members of the L.D.S. Church are also known as "Saints," a title which, when used in the Mormon Church, is applied to all members, and refers to membership alone, and not to any personal achievement or virtue.

As soon as the Church was organized in 1830, the Mormons were persecuted, being driven in turn from Ohio to Missouri to Illinois. Finally, after Joseph Smith was murdered by an angry mob while he was imprisoned in a jail at Carthage, Illinois, the Latter-day Saints were expelled from the confines of the United States into the western frontier. Brigham Young assumed the leadership of the L.D.S. Church, and led the first band of pioneers across the plains to the high valleys of the Rocky Mountains, to an area eventually to become known as Utah. With their membership now scattered across the continent, and their numbers decimated by disease, starvation, and bloody massacres in Missouri, the Mormon leaders gave renewed emphasis to missionary work both in the United States and abroad. As new converts joined the faith, they were encouraged to gather in "Zion," the Saints' new home in Utah.

When Savage was introduced to the Mormon religion in 1848, the first band of pioneers was struggling to found a community in the wilderness of the Rocky Mountains. The missionaries in England, most of whom had left their families back in the United States in near poverty, were actively searching for people interested in learning about the church. Prejudice against the Mormon faith ran high in England, fueled by the rumors common in the American

newspapers. Few parents in England wanted their children to join this strange new religion, which threatened to pull their sons and daughters to a distant land. Savage's parents were no exception. His decision to join the Mormon Church led to difficult times at home, and family tradition states that he was disowned by his father. Later letters from his brother George reflect no bad feelings between the family members,[4] but he seldom spoke about his family in later life, and the full effect of his conversion on his family life is unknown. Savage chose to be baptized on the evening of May 25, 1848. He stated that he "had a hard struggle to get away with the clothes necessary to be babtised in, as I was closely watched by my Brother." Despite his family's efforts to prevent his baptism, he met his friend Fred Rogers, "after being chased from one street to another." The two of them proceeded to the "hole off Southampton Quay," where they were submerged in the cold waters by Elder John Lewis. Savage later wrote:

Never will I forget the Impression made upon my mind the few moments we knelt together in fervent prayer previous to babtizm. The tears rolled down my cheeks as the fervent prayers of that Man of God were sent to Heaven. It was as it were the first dawning of heavenly light in my dark soul, never before did I realize the beauty of prayer to the extent that I did that night; never before in my short pilgrimage in this stage had my knees been bent in such earnest supplication as on that occasion. I truly felt that there was a spirit in the work in which I was about to engage that was worth the reception. I felt from that time determined to serve the Lord with all my heart.

FIGURE 5.
Portrait of Joseph Smith by Gittins. Property of L.D.S. Museum of Church History and Art.

On the following Sunday he was confirmed a member of the L.D.S. Church. As part of the blessing of confirmation given to him at that time, he was promised that a speech impediment that had troubled him from his youth would be removed. Savage later felt that this blessing, along with many others promised in the prayer, had been completely fulfilled.

Charles was unemployed at this time, and this created great difficulty for him, as did the constant friction at home over his church membership. When his Mormon friend and teacher T. B. H. Stenhouse found work for him on the Isle of Wight, just off the southern coast of England, he jumped at the chance. He moved away

FIGURE 6.
Lithograph entitled
"The Martyrdom of Joseph Smith,
Carthage, Illinois, July 27, 1844."
Property of L.D.S. Museum of
Church History and Art.

from home to begin his new job at "Fishmonger, Etc." in the employ of a "Brother Lewis" (apparently a different man than the Lewis who baptized him). The exact nature of Savage's job at "Fishmonger, Etc." is uncertain. Soon after he began working there, an L.D.S. missionary named Paul Harrison arrived with his wife, assigned to what was known as the Newport Branch. According to Savage, Harrison soon "lost the Spirit, and then the work ceased." Savage spent part of his spare time preaching in the streets with Harrison and "a Brother named Shaw from Leeds, whom Paul babtized Illegally." He described having "many escapes from the fury of the crowd," and on one occasion was given a severe beating. They "managed to get hold of two of the crowd and had them before the magistrates for which they were fined eight pounds or eight days imprisonment."

Persecution continued against the small group of Saints and this, in combination with the poor business dealings of Lewis, led to financial problems at Fishmonger, Etc. Eventually Lewis "ran away with a Sister that was in the Newport Branch," and the entire business collapsed. The remaining partners were left with the debts, totaling more than one hundred pounds. They sold the company's assets, settled accounts as best they could, and left the Isle of Wight. Charles later wrote:

> The once glorious prospects of the Newport Branch were blasted and through the unwise proceedings of Paul during his stay there it has blasted the work in the island for a long time. Thus has the unwise proceedings of a man caused the work to stand still. If he had kept the commandments of the Lord he would have had a fine branch there.

Charles left the Isle of Wight with Harrison, Sister Lewis, and several other Saints, bound for Manchester. When he arrived in Southampton, however, he met his friend Stenhouse, who counseled him to stay there and avoid association with his former Newport Branch companions. This advice was well founded, for he later learned that his former partners had been excommunicated from the Church, and became bitter opponents of Mormonism.

Once again penniless and out of work, the young Mormon convert struggled to survive in Southampton. In the summer of 1851 Stenhouse and another friend, Brother Dunbar, introduced him to a Portsmouth shop owner, William Eddington, and persuaded the merchant to give Savage a job in his stationery and book store. This was another turning point in Savage's life. William Eddington was a prominent citizen in Portsmouth, and soon after joining the L.D.S. Church in 1850 was made the president of the Portsmouth Branch. He was an intelligent, educated man who was well known for his many acts of kindness to his fellow men. The cultured Englishman not only gave Savage a job, but took on the task of educating this raw, illiterate youth. Despite his lack of formal education, Savage had a sharp, active mind, and made considerable intellectual progress during the year and a half he spent with Eddington. The knowledge and refinement acquired in this arrangement had a lasting effect on him, and caused him to write in later years: "I shall ever cherish with fond remembrance the memory of Bro. Eddington who took me as it were out of the dust and placed me as it were on the road to fame." Savage's association with the Eddingtons was not merely educational. The Eddingtons took the young man into their family, providing the lov-ing family circle he had lost when he joined the church. They remained life-long friends, and Savage always spoke fondly of Mrs. Eddington, who was "as good as a mother to me."[5]

In the winter of 1852, William Eddington sold his store and headed for New York, en route to Utah to join the Mormon colony. Savage, meanwhile, had a different road to travel.

NOTES

1. For a complete genealogy of the Savage family, see appendix A.
2. Savage, "Life History," manuscript. Unless otherwise cited, all quotations in this chapter have been excerpted from this source.
3. "Sister Clench," to Marianne Clark Sharp, 1966, regarding her grandfather, Henry Puzey. In Savage Book of Remembrance.
4. See letters in Savage Book of Remembrance.
5. Savage Journals, December 31, 1887.

TRUTH WILL F

THE LATTER-DAY SAINTS

WILL HOLD **TWO**

MEETINGS

ON CHESTER GREEN,

DERBY,

On SUNDAY, Aug. 12th, 1855,

Commencing at half-past 10 a.m., and 6 o'clock p.m., (weather permitting,)

Otherwise at their MEETING ROOM, TOP of PARK STREET,

When the following ELDERS will be present;—

ISRAEL EVANS,

(From GREAT SALT LAKE CITY, UTAH,)

C. R. SAVAGE

(Lately returned from a Mission to Switzerland,)

Who, with OTHER ELDERS expected will ADDRESS the MEETING upon their

FAITH AND DOCTRINES.

"*To the law and to the testimony:* if they speak not according to this word it is because there is no light in them."—ISAIAH viii. 20.

"They that have truth ask no favour, save that of being heard; they dare the judgement of mankind."—G. J. HOLYOAKE.

CHAPTER 2

The Call of Zion

THE next stage of Savage's life began when he was ordained to the priesthood office of an elder in the Portsea Branch.[1] He was also assigned to work as the secretary to G. Bramwell, president of the Southampton Conference.[2] His duties in this office included traveling on foot between the various branches of the conference, collecting donations from church members. He kept careful accounts of the "receipts" from the Redlynch, Salisbury, and Southampton branches, as well as a journal of his activities. His journal recounts his efforts as a part-time missionary, working at times with the full-time missionaries or "traveling elders." He apparently had no job in this period, and was supported at least in part by donations from local church members. He worked hard in his duties as secretary, and earned the respect of his associates.

Late in 1853, Savage met with Apostle Franklin D. Richards, then president of the European branch of the L.D.S. Church. He was assigned the job of a fulltime missionary, and told to travel to Geneva, Switzerland, to report to his old friend Stenhouse, who was serving at that time as president of the Swiss Mission. On November 25, Savage left his homeland for France, on his way to Geneva. Once in Switzerland, he set to work learning the French language and preaching the Gospel. He traveled great distances throughout Switzerland on foot, part of the time in company with Elder William Budge, an old acquaintance from his days in the Southampton Conference. In Switzerland, the missionaries suffered much of the same persecution that they had experienced in England, and at one time he and Budge were imprisoned for three days in Zurich for preaching.

A year later, the Swiss Mission was combined with the Italian Mission, and President Stenhouse left for New York. Savage remained in Switzerland to continue his work with the new president, Daniel Tyler. At the close of his mission, he prepared a report of his labors for President Tyler. A small part of this report still exists, copied into the Savage scrapbook by some of his descendants, but this is the only available information on this period of his life. After spending nineteen months in Europe, Charles was honorably released to return to England.[3] This continental mission helped round out his education, and he returned to his native land a cultured gentleman, speaking fluent French and some German. At twenty-three, he was now an accomplished public speaker and a dedicated church representative.

Upon his return to England, Charles was assigned as a traveling missionary in the Derbyshire Conference, with Israel Evans. One day, while staying at the mission home in London, he was introduced to a young lady named Annie Adkins. Annie was an L.D.S. member from Luton, England, who had come to London for a church conference with a family friend, Brother Flitton. Young Annie was attracted to "Curly" Charley Savage, but he mistakenly believed that she was Brother Flitton's sweetheart, and did not pursue the relationship. Upon learning otherwise, he

FIGURE 7. (OPPOSITE)
Poster for meeting where C. R. Savage was to speak as a missionary. From Savage Scrapbook.

began to write to Annie, and their romance blossomed through the mail.

Annie had been a member of the Mormon faith since age sixteen. Her grandfather, John Fenn, had been one of the first to open his home to L.D.S. missionaries in Eaton Bray, Bedfordshire, and was baptized in 1847. At the age of seventy-five he quit England to join some of the Saints in Missouri. Annie's mother, Hannah Fenn Adkins, joined the church in 1852, followed a month later by her only daughter, Annie.[4] Two of Annie's brothers, Robert and Thomas, were also baptized, but her youngest brother, James, took after their father, Robert Adkins. A coach painter in Luton, Robert had no desire to join this strange new religion, and even less inclination to follow his father-in-law to America. Hannah knew, therefore, that she would never join her fellow Saints in America, but the desire to emigrate burned brightly in the heart of her only daughter. The United States was a beacon to Annie and to most of the English Saints, representing an opportunity to escape the bitter persecution leveled against the Mormons in England. Emigration was seen by the English members as a literal fleeing out of Babylon to the Promised Land. In order to accommodate and encourage this gathering movement toward "Zion," Church leaders established the Perpetual Emigration Fund. Under this system, poorer members could travel to the New World at church expense, although they were required to provide their own meals, bedding, and personal items. Once settled in Utah, these members were expected to repay the debt, thereby providing funds for the next group of emigrants. During the years it was in operation, the P.E.F. assisted thousands of families to relocate to the American West.

Hannah expected and even encouraged her daughter to emigrate. She had not foreseen the arrival of this handsome young suitor from the Derbyshire Conference and was initially suspicious of him, but her fears were soon quieted by the good reports of Charles she received from local members. Although he had immediately fallen in love, Annie appears to have been less easily convinced. At one point, Annie wrote to him, explaining she had planned on moving to the Valley of the Great Salt Lake, and had always imagined going as a single woman. She also expressed some doubts regarding marriage at that time, and declared that she must have the utmost confidence in the man she was to marry. Charles replied in an undated letter:

> I believe that in matters of this sort we should seek the Spirit of Heaven to guide us, and we should never make a choice unless we believe that it would conduce to our happiness. I chose Annie from witnessing many little traits in her character which suited my natural temperament and those traits I thought would accord exactly with mine. You say you would not like to promise unless you had full confidence in the object of your choice above all other men. Now Annie, confidence is a thing that comes with time and as you know very little of me I hope you will have the charity to try whether CRS is not worthy of that confidence you speak of. This much I think you believe of me; that I love this work and that I am ready to do anything for it. Whatever else you want to learn about me, time and intercourse will show.[5]

In the fall of 1855 Savage visited Annie in Luton, winning not only her heart, but her

FIGURE 8.
Annie Adkins Savage as a young woman, c. 1868.
Collection of Harrison Brothers.

THE SAVAGE VIEW

mother's approval as well. The young couple set to work planning for their future together, but on December 5 Charles was notified to report to the Liverpool office for yet another assignment. He was appointed as interpreter for a group of Italian Saints, many of whom spoke French, who were traveling to America under the auspices of the Perpetual Emigration Fund. His fare was to be paid by the church, but there were no funds available for Annie. He was scheduled to leave in five days aboard the John J. Boyd.

He hurriedly sent his pocket watch to Annie as a keepsake, placed one pound on an account with the Perpetual Emigration Fund in Annie's name, and gathered together a few necessities for the voyage. He boarded the vessel on December 10, 1855, with one pound in his pocket to sail to his Promised Land. Before the ship cast off, he wrote a final letter to his sweetheart:

On Board the "John J. Boyd" River Mersey Sunday Night at 10 Dec. 1855
    My dear Annie
    From the vessell I write to you, some are praying, some are fixing their goods; children crying, some getting in bed and some walking about forming a very curious and interesting sight. Your humble servant is second Counsellor to the Presidency of the Ship. I am along with 2 or 3 Scotch families. My company of Italians are not far off. They are not a very bright sample, but they are good, honest hearted souls; I am messing with the Scotch Saints. They are very kind and attentive to me. I have held two meetings tonight, one in French, and one in English. A real good spirit prevailed in the meeting and they all expressed themselves as determined to carry out all the suggestions. The President

of the ship is Elder Petersen. He has the charge of 400 and odd Saints from Denmark. I have to look after the English and the Italians. The Danish brethren appear to be fine men. The women are nothing extra. I think this is about all I can say at present. I may just mention that I am sleeping between two married couples but I don't feel very bashful as there is no time for that. You have to look out and not lose your traps. I am pretty comfortable. I was so hurried that I could not get all I might have had had I had more time to get ready in, but all is right with me. I have regretted many times that you were not here, as I find it is as cheap to make a calculation for 2 as one. . . .
    I must now close. The time is not far off before I will have to be on the deep, deep sea. Pray for me then my dear that I may have a safe and speedy voyage and that I may be able faithfully to carry out the responsibilities that rest upon me.
    Kindest love to your Mother, Bro. Flitton, and all the Saints, and accept the same yourself from your Affectionate Charley.
    I will write from the West. In the meantime "Trim your lamp and keep it burning."

This was the beginning of Savage's adventurous voyage across the Atlantic. The crossing made by the John J. Boyd was one of the roughest recorded in that period, and several emigrants died during the passage. Years later, he described the trip in a talk to a group of young people in Salt Lake City. His account provides some fascinating insights about travel in the days of the great sailing ships.[6]
    We left Liverpool on the tenth day of December 1855 on a sailing ship named the

John J. Boyd, a staunch vessel of some 2500 tons. After fixing up our berths, hanging up our cooking utensils and putting things in order generally, the time came to say good-bye to Old England which we did with many heart-aches.

A steam tug hauled us out to the British Channel. Sails were then unfurled and we were heading for the Great Atlantic Ocean. Everything seemed smooth and pleasant up to this time. Later on the ship's motion began to affect the passengers, then the fun began. The scene that followed would be hard to describe, in fact, better left alone.

In those days when freight ships carried passengers her main and lower decks were changed so that bunks could be constructed around the sides to hold one or two in a bunk as the case might be. They were built across the deck with the heads near the sides of the vessel. The only light came from the upper deck. Passengers were required to furnish their own mattresses, bedding, their cooking utensils, in fact, all that was needed for use on the voyage.

There were no divisions between the bunks. Simply boards that were high enough to keep one from falling out onto his next neighbor when the ship pitched; when it rolled you were compelled to set your feet hard against the foot board to keep from slipping out onto the deck.

We had 509 Saints aboard, 437 were from Denmark, Sweden, and Norway, 30 from Piedmont, Italy, and 42 from Great Britain. It was quite a job to stow them all away to give each one a bunk. The married couples were put into one section. The unmarried men and women in sections by themselves.

Our cooking utensils were stowed beneath the bunks and everything was done to make the most of very poor accommodations.

For our diet we had very hard ship biscuit. These we soaked in tea or soup as the case might be. They were made from graham flour and were warranted to keep for ages. Our meat was alternatively salt pork or beef. We had some potatoes and rice, sugar, and tea were also furnished. There were no tables for use. Our boxes were the only apology. They served for seats as well. We had to take our turns at the cook's galley and it often proved a trying ordeal to cook what we needed.

The Saints were not long getting acquainted. All were happy in the thought that they were going to Zion. We had prayers night and morning; when the weather permitted which was very seldom. Our whole voyage was a stormy one. The very first night out will be hard for me to forget. My bunk was between two married couples. One was from Scotland the other a Bro. Loader and wife, were from London. An elderly couple were also near. The old lady kept up a continuous complaint at her husband all the night through. Our ship rolled and pitched. The oil lamps made it dim and sepulchral. Above was the roar of the wind and the swishing of the waves. Below, where we were, was the darkness and terrible confusion. Our boxes went sliding around the deck, lurching all night long. Our tins and pans broke loose from their places and tumbled about everywhere making a noise equal to the roar above. The dim light of the lantern served to heighten the effect of the confusion produced by the storm. The passengers were badly frightened. Some screamed out, some cried, some grumbled and some prayed. All did something for the conditions were new and terrifying in the extreme, to those of us who were taking our first ocean voyage.

When the morning returned we collected our things, retied our boxes and fastened our tins. We did our best to restore order. The Saints crawled out of their berths and helped in the restoration. Sunshine came and with it a change of feeling from the experience of the night before. Thus the days wore on, sometimes fair wind but more frequently foul weather. We who were well enough to get up on the deck watched the waves and looked for ships, doing anything and everything to wear away the time.

On one occasion we were visited by a terrible hurricane, so bad that we could not carry any sails at all. The saints were terribly frightened. The rolling of the ship and the deafening roar of the wind through the ship's rigging will never be forgotten by me. Many of the saints fell on their knees in prayer at the same time holding on to keep from sliding around. I had the curiosity to go up on deck to witness the effects of the gale. Imagine my feelings, when near the top of the stairway in a little sort of cabin, I saw four or five of the sailors playing a game of cards to pass away the time. I felt there could not be such great danger even in this terrible storm if these old weather-worn sailors could sit calmly playing cards.

At one time we espied a large vessel rolling about with her masts broken off. I saw the American flag reversed which is the sign that the captain wanted help. Our vessel was slowed down and boats put off to bring the sailors from the wrecked ship. She proved to be the Louis Napoleon from Baltimore loaded with flour. The captain and crew were brought to our vessel and the big ship left to the mercy of the waves. Our own crew were getting badly used up with the constant bad weather. The rescued sailors proved a help in need to our captain.

One of the disagreeable features we noticed was the cruelty of this captain and mates toward the common sailors. Harshness, coarseness, and inhumanity seemed the only sentiments in their conduct. A good many of the Danish saints died on the ship owing to the continued bad weather and the lack of proper facilities to care for the sick. The voyage was a long tempestuous one lasting from the 10th of December 1855 to the 27th of Feb. 1856. Possibly no company of saints ever experienced a more trying ordeal than those who crossed on the John J. Boyd. There was only one day's supply of water left when we landed in New York. We all felt to thank God for our safe arrival.

On arrival in New York, the Saints from the John J. Boyd were housed in a large hall in Williamsburg. The winter of 1855-56 was severe, with deep snow and bitter cold. Elder John Taylor, later to become the third president of the L.D.S. Church, was at that time living in New York, publishing a periodical called *The Mormon*. He arranged for the new immigrants to shovel snow, thus enabling them to earn money to support their families through the harsh winter. Savage found a home with his friend Stenhouse and his wife, who were "roughing it without either chairs or tables, but these are small matters when contentment and peace

reign supreme."[7]

As spring neared, the Italian immigrants moved westward to join the Saints in the Rocky Mountains. Charles stayed in New York and spent at least part of his time working in the office of *The Mormon*. In a letter to Annie, he described how he was getting along. "Now with regard to myself and my prospects," he wrote, "I can say that I am in first-rate health and spirits. . . . I have every prospect of doing well, but cannot just now say what I am going to do. Suffice it to say all will be right with me, and will still be more so in a few months."

He also expressed his concern to his sweetheart over his inability to raise the money necessary to bring her to America. His late arrival in New York and the harsh winter combined to delay his plans for sending her the needed funds, and because of the poverty of the local church members he was unable to borrow the money. However, he did have a plan:

On my part I told you I left one pound to your account on the books in Liverpool. Now I will tell you how I think you can manage it to make up the rest. I left my watch which I hoped you would keep for my sake. Well, you can pawn it for 1 pound or 30 shillings very easily. You can then sell the ticket for another pound which will make you 2 in all. This with the pound will be 3 possibly. As you are not coming out in January or February you may be able to save a few shillings. This with what I can get forwarded to you from one or two quarters will enable you to reach this place. When here you can find your humble servant. . . . I will pay anybody good interest for what they may do for you.

After reflecting that "New York is a queer place, and the people are queerer still," he gave Annie some interesting advice on how to plan for her trip:

Now a little counsel on how to get along. When you come bring with you a few figs, plums, or raisins, some baking powder, get as good a bed as you can. Straw is a hard thing to lie upon when the vessel rolls. A few extra potatoes and some flour, also some bags of different sizes to put your provisions in. Take care of them every week. They are very valuable here. You can sell them very easy or they will be very useful. Bring jam or ham or anything you can eat but let me say one word. Keep them in your box until you get hungry and badly. Don't take them out until then. Many Saints eat all the nice things they had before they really wanted them. Bring a pound or two of butter. You will get tired of biscuits soon and will find them hard nuts to crack. Therefore anything nice will go down better. Bring a half pint earthenware cup. Never mind about the tin ones. Tea and water drink better out of them than the tin ones. The same may be said of plates. Get a knife and fork, a small iron pot to cook with and stone jars to keep your water in, if not a tin one will do. Take care to have your boxes, jars, tins and everything well fastened. Look to this. Let them be so packed that you can get at them easily. See that they cannot slide either to the right or the left. A tin wash hand basin, a pound of candles, a box or two of matches, another word with you. Come with Brother M. You need not trouble about anything but what you want yourself, there will be light enough from his candles to light you. All items are good if you have got cash. If short, never mind it is better for you to have money on your arrival here than spend it all on luxuries. Personal necessities you must not forget. A little soap will be useful. . . . The hints in my letter will suit anybody so don't be afraid to show them.

Praying God to bless you continually, I am as ever, Yours Affectionately, C. R. Savage

P.S. I will send you a specimen soon of what I am doing in the City of New York.[8]

Soon thereafter, he wrote his sweetheart to inform her that a new friend in New York would advance him the means to send for her. On April 30, 1856, Annie bid goodbye to her friends and family, on her way to the New World. She traveled to Dunstable in a pony cart, where she took the train to Liverpool. A few days later she boarded the sailing ship Thornton, which she described as "large and very fine." Annie kept a journal during her voyage to New York, which provides fascinating glimpses of sea travel in that era.[9]

In contrast to Charley's passage, the weather during Annie's trip was excellent. The voyage was not without its share of excitement, however. Midway through the trip, an over-heated stove in the galley started a small fire. The emigrants carried water in pails, and the blaze was soon extinguished. By the time the good ship Thornton hove in sight off the New York coast on June 14, there had been three burials, three weddings, and four babies born aboard her. The captain of the vessel had never traveled with Mormons before, and both he and the ship's surgeon were impressed by their organization, cleanliness, and contentment. He loved to hear Mormon hymns sung, and would often request his favorites. Annie noted in her journal that, at the end of the journey, the captain told his passengers that he would never forget that trip with the Mormon emigrants.

On June 24, just ten days after Annie's arrival in New York City, the young couple were married in Brooklyn. Elder John Taylor performed the ceremony, which was witnessed by W. H. Miles, George A. Smith, Orson Pratt, Ezra T. Benson, and Erastus Snow.[10]

Charles and Annie soon moved into new quarters on the corner of Second and Sixth streets in Williamsburg, New York. Charles was working at this time in Samuel Booth's printing office, and paying off the debts incurred in bringing himself and his bride to New York. His journal suggests that he was still struggling financially, and he worked at various jobs, including moving furniture and selling magazine subscriptions.[11] Annie had been trained to make straw hats in Luton, and was an excellent seamstress; her skills helped keep the couple solvent. It was an exciting time in New York, with the Saints renting large halls to accommodate crowded church meetings. Savage's journal records that he was placed in charge of the New

FIGURE II.
Daguerreotype portrait of Charles Savage, c. 1857, published in Deseret Evening News, *July 8, 1916.*

York Branch Choir, and also participated in a few plays and music festivals.

A year and a month after their marriage, Annie bore her first child, a boy. Charles Stenhouse Savage was hurriedly named and blessed seventeen days later because they feared that he would not survive. Their fears were confirmed, and the child died of cholera at the age of five months, and lies buried in Union Cemetery. This was a tremendous blow to Annie, so far from home and family. Hoping that a change of scenery would help, Charles sent his grieving young wife to the country to stay with a friend's family. After her return, the couple moved to 186 East 36th Street in New York. The following June their second son, Roscoe Eddington Savage, was born, helping to fill the void left by the loss of their first child.

Savage's journals are difficult to follow during these busy days in New York, and much information for this segment of his life is obtained from family tradition and letters written between the couple. After his arrival in New York, he re-used his 1855 pocketbook to write notes on matters both financial and photographic, possibly because he was too poor to buy new pocketbooks. This one journal, therefore, comprises his notations for the years 1855, 1856, 1857, and 1858. Since the dates are often incomplete, it is sometimes difficult to determine when an event took place.

It was clearly during these early days in New York, however, that Savage was first introduced to the art of photography. His friend Stenhouse had brought a stereoscope camera with him from England, and in their spare time the two young men experimented with its use. Some family histories written of Savage have claimed that these were the first stereoscope pictures pro-

duced in the United States.[12] Charles himself, in a later writing, was less ambitious, claiming only that they were the first stereographs made on Long Island. At one point during the course of these experiments they "got stuck," and appealed to a photographer on Broadway for help, "which he graciously did at the rate of five dollars per hour for instructions."[13]

There is some uncertainty regarding where Charles received his photographic training. As an avid reader, he could certainly have picked up the process through the journals of the day, with plenty of trial and error. Family histories of Charles and Annie Savage, written by two of his descendants, stated that he learned the art from Stenhouse, who "was one of the leading photographers of that time,"[14] and "had a photograph gallery in Brooklyn."[15] Savage's journals do indeed reflect time spent with Stenhouse in photographic pursuits as early as April of 1856.

A conflicting report is contained in a biographical sketch by Ruby Clayson of Edward Covington, another English-born Mormon convert, who arrived in New York on January 1, 1857. This account states that C. R. Savage served as an apprentice under Covington in the photographic business. Covington was only in New York a few months, however, before he left for Utah in the train of Johnston's Army in August of 1857. This fact, along with Savage's journal entries showing early training in the art in 1856, tends to discount this single report. Several years after Savage's death, a photograph came to light that further clouds the issue.

This photograph, shown in figure 11, was a daguerreotype purportedly taken in New York in 1856 "by an artist named Covington." In 1857 Charles gave it to Dr. Matthew McCune, another of his close friends. This image is the earliest known portrait of Savage, and was identified among Dr. McCune's papers after his death. The identification was confirmed by an entry in Dr. McCune's journal, "where he referred to the occasion and circumstances under which the picture had been presented to him." This photograph and the accompanying story were published in a Salt Lake newspaper in 1916.[16] Unfortunately, both the original daguerreotype and Dr. McCune's 1857 journal have since been lost.

Therefore, although Savage apparently received much of his early training in photography in company with Stenhouse, he did have some contact with Edward Covington. To further confuse the question, a review of business directories of Brooklyn and other New York areas shows no sign of a photograph gallery run by either Stenhouse or Covington during the period of 1855-58. In all likelihood, Savage received instruction from several individuals, and the notes in his journals suggest a wide range of reading on the subject as well.

Regardless of the source of his photographic training, his journal is full of notes to himself on various formulas for developing, toning, and fixing solutions, as well as notations of photographic equipment bought. The portrait photographers of the 1850s were just making the transition from daguerreotypes to the collodion processes of the ambrotype, tintype, and glass-plate negatives for paper prints. Savage had notes regarding each of these newer methods in his journal, and later records show that he became proficient in all of them.

Charles continued to work at Samuel Booth's printing office until 1859, when he was called by Elder George Q. Cannon to go alone to Florence, Nebraska, on church business. This concluded, he sent for his wife and son to join him at Council Bluffs, Iowa, the jumping-off point for most overland wagon trains at that time. With him he had brought his view cameras and chemicals, with all the necessary equipment to embark on his new career of photography.

NOTES

1. Ordination certificate, Savage Book of Remembrance.
2. Savage Missionary Journal, Savage Book of Remembrance.
3. Letter of release from mission signed by Mission President Daniel Tyler. Copy in Savage Book of Remembrance.
4. Sharp.
5. This and other letters in this chapter from Savage to Annie Adkins exist as handwritten copies in the Savage Book of Remembrance.
6. Savage, "An Ocean Voyage in a Sailing Ship," manuscript, Savage Scrapbook; two other accounts of this trip by Savage may be found in his 1856 Journal and in Jenson, 106-107.
7. Savage, New York City, to Annie Adkins, undated. Handwritten copy in Savage Book of Remembrance.
8. This may refer to Savage's early attempts at photography.
9. Some excerpts from this journal are included in Sharp's "Life History of Annie Adkins." The location of the original journal is not known to the author.
10. Clark, *Life Sketch of Charles Rosecoe Savage*.
11. Savage Journals, February 20, March 24, 1855.
12. Clark, *Life Sketch of Charles Rosecoe Savage*.
13. Savage, "A Photographic Tour," p. 313.
14. Clark, *Life Sketch of Charles Rosecoe Savage*.
15. Sharp.
16. "Leaves from Old Albums," Deseret Evening News, July 8, 1916.

CHAPTER 3

Across the Plains

ONCE settled in Council Bluffs, Iowa, Charles opened his photographic business. It was primitive, even by the standards of that time. A tent, a gray blanket for a backdrop, and an old wooden tea-chest for a darkroom comprised his studio. The immigrants crowding through Council Bluffs on their way to "Zion," although poor, wanted portraits of their family members. They paid Savage with whatever they had, including food and other supplies. Business was fairly good, and during a four-month period the young photographer cleared $224.75 for taking portraits, with an additional $50 "for giving instructions in the art."[1] By June, the Savage family was able to buy a team and wagon and outfit it for the trip west.

On June 7, 1860, Charles and his young family were ferried across the river from Council Bluffs to Florence, Nebraska. The following day they joined a company of ten wagons under the leadership of Brother Franklin Brown, and started across the Great Plains. Three more wagons joined the group in the evening. The trip across the plains took two and one-half months. Other trains of wagons and hand cart companies were also moving along the old Mormon Trail. The hand cart companies were organized by the Perpetual Emigration Fund as a more economical method of bringing converts to Utah. Although pushing a large cart loaded with supplies and family possessions across the plains must have been exhausting, the hand-cart companies generally kept pace with the full wagon trains. On several occasions during this trip across the plains, pioneers from the hand cart company came to the wagon train to buy flour or obtain help for their sick and injured.[2]

At one point in the journey the train came upon another train of "32 wagons from Salt Lake and 42 Missionaries,"[3] led by Joseph W. Young (one of President Brigham Young's sons). This group of ox-drawn wagons was one of the first of a series headed east to send missionaries off to destinations around the world. The ox-team trains were instituted in 1860 as an alternative to the relatively expensive and inefficient wagon and hand cart companies. Wagon teams available for purchase in Nebraska by pioneers were becoming increasingly limited and expensive. These wagons and stock, once driven to Utah, were worth considerably less than their purchased value, because of the large numbers available from arriving emigrants. To avoid depleting the Perpetual Emigration Fund's limited budget, the idea of two-directional traffic across the plains with ox teams was developed. The trains would carry missionaries and locally produced items to the East, where they could pick up a return load of emigrating Saints and eastern freight. After initial attempts in 1859 and 1860, the ox teams were considered a great success. Joseph Young gave a sermon in the Salt Lake Tabernacle to describe "ox-teamology,"[4] and it became the preferred method of overland transport for the Mormons until the coming of the railroad in 1869.[5] Often single young men volunteered to drive the ox teams east to pick up immigrants

FIGURE 12. (OPPOSITE)
Artist's rendering of a pioneer photographer's working tent.

in the hopes of meeting a potential bride on the return trip, and many romances blossomed on these journeys. Savage's journal relates that Joseph Young, as the leading ecclesiastical authority present, made some change in the organization of a hand cart company also traveling westward before he separated to continue east.

Charles clearly loved the adventure of traveling across the plains, as evidenced by many of his journal entries. Some of these notations describe efforts made to catch fish or game, and list conditions encountered each day. All of the entries indicate great enthusiasm for this journey, despite the obvious hardships:

June 15 Wed. Camped during the day. A general loafing time and a hard struggle made to catch some fish. June 17 Fri. Camped this day owing to the ferry not being in running order. Was surrounded by numbers of the Pawnee indians, very peaceable but great beggars. Got moccasins, etc. June 18 Sat. Drove 4 miles further up the Fork and saw the hand cart train ferry across without accident. A jolly time generally, women and girls wading with the greatest gusto. June 27 Started on our journey but had not proceeded far when were requested to camp as a little stranger was about to be ushered into the world. Brother Steven's wife being safely delivered of a fine boy, some ineffectual efforts were made to shoot buffalo without success. Days travel 2 ½ miles. Myriads of mosquitoes. June 29 Wed. Left camp and got to Buffalo Creek, moved there with the hand-carts. Couldn't see any buffalo. Passed on and camped near a dry ravine without wood or water. In fact, there is no place to camp between the creek and where the road joins the river. Chips plenty, some little water in a slough on the top of a hill. 26 miles. July 15 Fri. Left camp and travelled to a few miles east of Chimney Rock a solitary column of rock standing perpendicular on a tapering cone of rock. Found good feed. At this point the country around is very barren except near the river. Held a meeting in the evening. The surrounding scenery is one of romantic grandeur. July 16 Sat. From a point below Chimney Rock we pushed on and nooned near the river, finally got east of Scott's Bluff and here got visited by the Sioux but in small numbers. Road splendid, easy to camp anywhere; chips tolerable plenty. In full view of the rock all the time. July 22 Fri. Started for the hills and got over a very rough stony road, very hilly and hard on the oxen's hooves. Camped by the Platte for nooning, feed better, many relics of broken wagons around. Started over the hills again and got some tremendous hard pulls and some very steep rocky gulch of the worst kind. Camped in a hollow, no running water but oxen water, feed good. July 29 Fri. Travelled about 8 miles this day on the 16 mile stretch and found splendid feed among some timber after passing over the sand hills. We also discovered that one of Bro. Brown's oxen had been bitten by a rattle-snake, gave it whiskey and tobacco poultices. Plenty of wood, water, the best camping place we have found since leaving Scott's Bluff. Meeting in the evening. Aug 5 Fri. Got a splendid view of Devils Gate, a remarkable freak of nature.

The river trickles through a deep chasm of the rocks some 3 or 400 feet deep. Feed very good. The road in this section of country is kind of gravelly sand, hard on the hoofs. One of my oxen shows signs of getting a very sore neck. Aug 20 Sat. Open and pleasant. The Wasatch Mountains in the distance. Road tolerable this day after passing the 4th ford. The road is rather stony past Millersville this day, and saw hundreds of old wagons. The Road from Hams Fork to Bridger [is littered] with the bones of hundreds of cattle who died during the fuss with Utah,[6] camped about 2 miles east of Fort Bridger in good feed.

As seen in the above entries, Charles carefully noted traveling distances and conditions such as water, wood or "buffalo chips" for cooking fires, cattle feed, and road conditions. He had several "Guides," which were books describing the distances from each landmark and the expected traveling conditions for each portion of the overland trip. During the course of this trip he found a number of errors in these guides, especially in the distances between landmarks.[7] Several years later, he used the information gathered on this and other travels in the West to write a number of his own guide books. These guides, published as the railroad began to replace the wagon trains for overland travel, concentrated on the scenic opportunities available to tourists.

After weeks of travel, the wagon train wound down through the Weber Valley and Parley's Canyon to the Salt Lake Valley. Charles noted in his journal that he arrived in Salt Lake City at 10:00 p.m. on August 28. The following morning he found a temporary home for his

FIGURE 14.
Savage & Ottinger's second studio in Salt Lake City, c. 1864–70. Carte-de-visite, collection of Nelson Wadsworth.

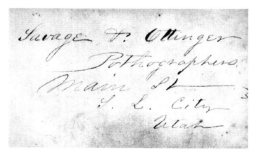

FIGURE 15.
Early imprint of Savage & Ottinger Studio from the reverse of a carte-de-visite, c. 1862. Collection of Carl Mautz.

family with his old friend William Eddington, and began looking for work. Within two days of reaching the Valley, the young cameraman entered into a business arrangement with Marsena Cannon, one of Salt Lake City's first daguerreotype photographers. Cannon's gallery was situated on East Temple in Salt Lake City. The partnership was intended to be temporary, since Marsena Cannon was planning to return to the East before long. Both partners shared equally in expenses and income. Cannon had already established a good reputation as a daguerreotype portrait artist, and even took some local city scenes using the extremely difficult medium of the daguerreotype. By 1860 he had successfully switched over to the newer wet-plate process.

Charles did well with Cannon as his partner. His journal reflects a steady business, although payment was often made in the form of poultry, molasses, beans, or other barter goods. Even whiskey and tobacco were given in trade for pictures. These items, although probably not used by Savage himself, could be resold or bartered for other goods. The "Word of Wisdom," the Mormon health code forbidding the consumption of harmful substances like tobacco and alcohol, was at that time a voluntary exercise rather than a mandatory rule, and many Mormons, especially the new immigrants, still used these products. In addition, whiskey and tobacco were both used extensively to make poultices for livestock. The photographers were glad to receive payment in any form during these difficult early years in Utah.

The oxen that had pulled Savage and his family across the plains were traded for a building lot on "the Bench," an area of Salt Lake City now known as "the Avenues." Charles began

building a house for his young family on this lot, later given the address of 80 D street. The five-room adobe structure was completed just in time to accommodate the arrival of the first little girl to join the family, Annie Amelia. The Savages settled into their new life in Utah with great contentment. Charles worked in partnership with Marsena Cannon until October 1861, when Cannon was assigned to move to southern Utah to help found the new colony of St. George, which was established to produce cotton for the territory. When the partnership dissolved, Savage continued working in the same studio on the east side of Main Street, between First and Second South. By 1862 he was joined by a new partner, 29-year old George Martin Ottinger, who had arrived in Utah only the year before.

George Ottinger was born in Springfield, Pennsylvania, of German parentage. His father wanted him to become a medical doctor, and refused to let young George study art as he desired, so Ottinger ran away from home to become a sailor. After several years at sea, visiting every continent as he circumnavigated the globe, Ottinger returned home. His parents, who had given him up for dead, made no further objection to his study of art, and he began studying under the artists of the Hudson River School. He joined the L.D.S. Church in Pennsylvania in 1858, and moved to Utah in 1861 with a hand cart company. Savage, who had known Ottinger's mother in the East,[8] suggested that the two men work together, with Savage doing photography and Ottinger tinting the photographs and painting miniature portraits. "I commenced coloring photographs, very poor ones at that, taken by C. R. Savage," Ottinger wrote in his journal. "The first picture I painted I received for pay two and a half gallons of molasses." Ottinger continued:

> Mr. Savage . . . had just started to make ambrotypes, photographs on glass, and was doing well in his work. He knew I could paint miniatures, and we soon became mutually interested in a photo and miniature business.
>
> We opened up a place as partners in the photograph business just north of the Deseret National Bank. It was a little one-story affair, and we soon decided to move. Mr. Savage then leased the spot of ground on which the present Savage establishment stands, just south of the Deseret News Building, and we moved our plant to that structure, where our business thrived.
> (*Deseret News*, January 22, 1916)

Utah in the 1860s was still very much part of the frontier. Although the settlements along the Wasatch Front and the mining towns in Nevada and Colorado were growing, Salt Lake City was really the only significant center of civilization between Nebraska and the West Coast. From the time of the first pioneers in 1847, Utah (initially called Deseret by the Mormons) had endured a series of financial and political setbacks. The early settlers suffered great privation as a result of the grasshopper plagues of 1855 and 1856, which decimated their crops. An unusually harsh winter in 1855 killed about two-thirds of the livestock in Utah. In addition to these natural disasters, there was a constant stream of new immigrants, all of whom needed to be fed and housed through the winter before becoming self-sufficient on their own farms. These factors combined to impoverish the inhabitants of the Great

Salt Lake Valley, but help arrived from a very unexpected source.

In early 1857, United States President Buchanan began a military action against the Mormon settlers in Utah. This military offensive, later known as the Utah War, was an attempt to bring order to a territory erroneously felt to be in a state of chaos and tyranny. When the troops arrived in Utah, they found the reports of disorder greatly exaggerated, and the Utah War ended peacefully, with no casualties. An agreement was made between the Federal troops and Mormon leaders in which the military could establish a camp no closer than forty miles to the city, but could not occupy the city itself.

The end of the Utah War signalled an era of unprecedented prosperity for the Latter-day Saints. Camp Floyd, as the base was dubbed, was described by Horace Greeley as "the largest regular force ever concentrated upon the soil of our country in a time of peace." With a population of four thousand Federal troops and three thousand non-military personnel, the camp provided a definite boost to the local economy. Farm produce, hay, straw, grain, lumber, blacksmithing, watch repair, and photography were all in demand by the troops. Church leaders organized price schedules to avoid competition and keep prices high. Toll gates were even erected along the wagon trails that served the area, and supply trains were charged for the privilege of entering the valley. When the Civil War broke out in July 1861, Camp Floyd was evacuated and the troops sent to more urgent assignments. All the camp's equipment was auctioned in what was the largest sale of government surplus up to that time. More than $4,000,000 of property was sold for about $100,000, prompting one church member to describe the incident as "the

FIGURE 16.
C. R. Savage on left and George Ottinger on right, c. 1864-1869 by an unknown photographer. Savage Book of Remembrance.

FIGURE 17.
Salt Lake City street scene. Carte-de-visite, c. 1860. Photo by C. R. Savage. Collection of L.D.S. Church Archives.

FIGURE 18.
*Painting by George M. Ottinger, "The Aztecs," c. 1865.
Collection of L.D.S. Church Museum of History
and Art.*

great Buchanan Expedition, costing the government millions, and accomplishing nothing, except making many of the Saints comparatively rich, and improving the circumstances of most of the people of Utah."[9]

The Third California Volunteers were sent to Utah to maintain a military presence in Salt Lake City for the dual purpose of protecting the settlers from Indian hostilities and keeping an eye on the Mormons. These troops, under the command of Colonel Patrick Connor, established Fort Douglas on the East Bench above Salt Lake City, and the lucrative trade of supplying commodities to the military continued.

When Charles began working with Cannon in 1860, the Utah settlers were still relatively prosperous from their trading with the military. Currency, however, was in short supply, since Utah still did little exporting to bring cash into

the Territory. This led to a flourishing barter system among the Saints. In addition to regular barter goods, the Mormons traded in "store-credit," that could be redeemed at the few local stores or at the Bishop's Store-house. The Bishop's Store-house was the repository for tithing receipts, or voluntary contributions to the church, which were also often paid in produce rather than cash.

With greater prosperity, it became possible for the Saints to afford artistic pursuits, and the arts began to flourish in Utah. This artistic movement was encouraged by church leaders both in sermons and in more practical ways, such as sending local artists to France to learn new painting and sculpture techniques. In 1861-62 the Mormons built the Salt Lake Theater, at a cost of $100,000. This structure, built on the model of the Drury Lane Theater of London, seated three thousand people, and was the first theater of importance west of the Mississippi.[10] It was preeminent throughout the nineteenth century, showcasing some of the best actors and actresses in the nation, and was a source of great civic pride for Utahns.

Savage and Ottinger were active members of their church and community, and both were soon taking leading roles in the artistic milieu in Utah. In 1863, a group of Salt Lake artists organized Utah's first art school, named the Deseret Academy of Art. Ottinger served as its first president, and Savage filled the post of treasurer. Many of Utah's early prominent artists served as officers or teachers in the Academy, which functioned for only a short time. It was superseded by the University of Deseret, the precursor to the present-day University of Utah. With

his easy-going, pleasant manner and natural concern for the welfare of others, Savage was a popular teacher.

During the next five years, both artists also became prominent businessmen in the Salt Lake City area. Ottinger began to paint local landscapes and paintings depicting scenes from the Book of Mormon, using sketches garnered from his earlier trips to Central and South America. He was commissioned by the L.D.S. Church to paint scenery for the Salt Lake Theater, and later assisted in painting murals in L.D.S. temples in Manti, Logan, and St. George. Savage dealt in portrait photography for Salt Lake citizens, but increasingly began exploring the wild, rocky canyons and ridges of Utah for scenic views to sell in the gallery. In fact, within four months of his arrival in Salt Lake City, he took

FIGURE 19.
"The Mormon Theatre taken before completion, December, 1865." Carte-de-visite by C. R. Savage. Collection of Carl Mautz.

a trip out to Camp Floyd, where he "took the store formerly occupied by Dryer Brothers." He stayed overnight at the saloon run by the infamous Porter Rockwell, the one-time bodyguard of the Prophet Joseph Smith, who was rumored to have killed several men in the discharge of this duty. While on this trip, Savage wrote of "passing several good spots for views of Utah Lake."[11]

He also did a lively business in photographs of the major buildings in Salt Lake City, for sale to both residents and tourists. These activities helped build the Savage and Ottinger Gallery financially, although the mainstay of the business in these early years was portrait photography. As his local renown as a portrait photographer grew, Savage was asked to take pictures of many of the leading men of Utah, including Brigham Young and his family.

The two young artists were also great patrons of the theater. In addition to painting scenery for the Salt Lake Theater, Ottinger often played supporting roles in local productions, as did Charles and Annie Savage. The studio of Savage and Ottinger became a regular outlet for the purchase of theater tickets. Savage's excellent singing voice, developed in the New York Branch choir, again came to the forefront when he joined the newly organized Mormon Tabernacle Choir as a charter member. He attended the practices faithfully, and at the time of his death was the oldest member of the choir, both in chronological age and in years served.

Charles was an active member of the 20th Ward of the L.D.S. Church, serving as an officer in the 20th Ward Institute and on its Board of Directors for many years, alongside friends such as Henry Purcey, Karl G. Maeser, G. W. Ottinger, and George Reynolds. Since the Institute was a non-ecclesiastical organization, leaders

FIGURE 20.
"Miss Alexander, leading lady of the Salt Lake City Theatre, trained by Brigham Young and his agent, Hiram Clawson." Carte-de-visite, c. 1865. Collection of Carl Mautz.

were elected rather than being appointed by church leaders, as was the case for most other positions. The members of the 20th Ward, including Savage, founded a "Literary Institute," where speakers on many subjects gave evening demonstrations or lectures. These lectures generally concerned scientific subjects, and, as his journals indicate, Charles was in great demand for talks on a surprising number of topics that included Africa, astronomy, geology, physics, photography, geography, and electricity. Other lectures were entitled "The Lewis and Clark Expedition," "The Mysteries of Light," and "Life on Other Worlds." On one occasion he supplemented his lecture with alarming scientific demonstrations:

> Lectured before the Twentieth Ward Institute to an audience of nearly 500 persons, men, women, and children, on *Light and Electricity* introducing for the first time the electric light and colored lights by means of the Rhunkoph Coil, with a battery of 35 cup. Fired guncotton on a stepladder, etc.[12]

The 20th Ward Literary Institute was a great success, and soon the idea spread to other local wards. Savage continued to present topics for years, long after he had ceased serving on the Board of Directors, and his journals frequently report traveling to other wards to speak on Sunday evenings, often in company with other speakers.

He also joined the Nauvoo Legion, a military unit first organized in Nauvoo, Illinois, as a branch of the Illinois State Militia, under a local charter. The Legion was created so that the Mormons could defend themselves against the systematic persecution by their neighbors in Illinois. After the Saints' expulsion from the United States and subsequent migration to Utah, the Nauvoo Legion was reformed, with many original members in its ranks. When the area became recognized as the Utah Territory, the band was renamed the "Militia of Utah Territory," although locals continued to refer to it as the Nauvoo Legion. On April 25, 1866, Charles was promoted to "1st Lieutenant of Infantry, 3rd Regiment, 1st Brigade, 1st Division, Great Salt Lake Military District, of the Militia of Utah Territory."[13] He was later promoted to Captain.[14] Ottinger was also a member of the Nauvoo Legion, along with many of Savage's other friends. The occasional monotony of frontier life was frequently interrupted by social activities such as military dress balls and legion drills, and Savage took an active part in them. In 1864, he also became a naturalized citizen of the United States, presumably before joining the Nauvoo Legion.[15]

The studio prospered under the hands of Savage and Ottinger, and soon the two young entrepreneurs had a thriving business. Charles traveled throughout Utah in search of photographic opportunities, and managed to keep his portrait photography business going as well.

The majority of photographers in the 1860s were simple studio photographers, supplying the demand for family and individual portraits in galleries across the nation. The collodion glass-plate negative, or "wet-plate," was a marked improvement over the daguerreotype for portrait photography. The greatly shortened exposure times made sitting for a portrait less arduous, while at the same time increasing the productivity of the photographer. The cheaper price of the photographs put family portraits within reach of the masses for the first time. Multiple copies of the same image could be produced, and the toxic mercury and iodine fumes of the daguerreotype process became a thing of the past. Despite these advantages, however, wet-plate photography was still a cumbersome process requiring exact chemistry and meticulous technique.

To prepare a wet-plate, the cameraman would clean a glass plate and then, inside a dark room or tent, pour collodion onto the center and tilt it to spread the collodion evenly. The excess was then poured off. When the collodion had dried to a tacky state, the plate was sensitized in a silver bath and placed in a light-tight holder. Only then could the plate be brought into the sunlight, where the exposure, lasting from five seconds to four minutes, could be made. The plate was then developed, fixed, washed, and dried. It was necessary to perform the entire process, from sensitizing the plate to development, before the plate dried and lost its sensitivity. The chemistry was fickle and subject to many variables, including temperature, humidity, and water impurities. The fumes from the ether and other chemicals within the confines of a small tent or wagon could be tolerated for only a short while, and added to the necessity for rapid work. The ether was also extremely flammable, and many a photographer's studio burned to the ground during the wet-plate era.

Because of these limitations, most wet-plate photographers preferred to remain in the studio where conditions were predictable. A few, like Savage, left the security of the studio to brave the difficulties of field photography. These frontier photographers were usually itinerants who traveled from place to place, searching for new vistas to capture on glass. Such men, though dedicated, were almost invariably poor. They

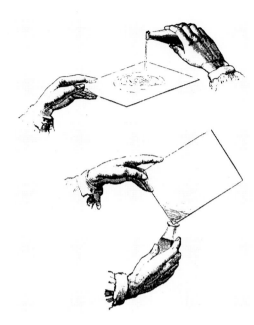

FIGURE 21.
Engraving depicting preparation of glass negative by the wet-plate collodion process.

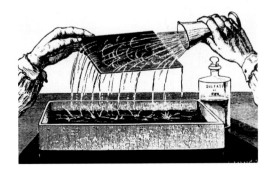

FIGURE 22.
Developing exposed glass negative by the wet-plate collodion process.

supported themselves by selling copies of their pictures along the way, or stopping in frontier towns to take portraits to raise money for a few more weeks of work. The lucky ones were supported by the railroads or by stereoscopic view distributors during their travels, but most only hoped to be able to sell their prints or negatives at the end of their trip through the frontier. This system, by its very nature, tended to limit the time a photographer could spend in the wilds.

Because of the relative newness of multiple print technology, copyright observance was erratic at best. Field photographers of that era commonly sold, loaned, or copied negatives, and the resulting prints were often sold without crediting the original photographer. Only years later did copyright observance for photographs approach that of written material. Although they were considered artists, frontier cameramen were often financially at the mercy of large photographic distributors or other organizations. In the 1860s and 1870s, a photographer could usually sell his prints locally, but a distributor was necessary to reach the lucrative national market. Most frontier photographers preferred being in the field, and had neither the aptitude nor the time to market their own photos, at least for any extended period. Therefore they often sold their negatives to a large stereoscopic producer for distribution and sale.

Charles Savage was an exception to this rule. Salt Lake City was in the heart of the scenic frontier, allowing him to photograph landscapes on short trips with a minimum of expense. His studio provided a stable financial base as well as a ready market for his views, allowing him to sell only the prints and retain control of the negatives. He also possessed considerable business ability, and found many ways to promote his business locally. He advertised frequently in the Salt Lake newspapers, and often tried innovative approaches to advertising and sales. At one point, noticing that he had taken many children's portraits over the years, he created a composite picture of children's faces, entitled "Utah's Best Crop," and sold as many copies as he could. Of course, the families of every child in the picture wanted at least one copy. This tactic was apparently successful, since Charles repeated it with different children several times.

His newspaper advertisements reflect the wide variety of photographs taken in the studio in these early days.[16] Ambrotypes, melainotypes (tintypes), stereoviews, carte-de-visites, miniature photographs, locket pictures, life-size portraits, and tinted photos in both watercolors and oils were all offered to the clientele of Savage and Ottinger. Many of these methods gradually fell into disuse, as the public demanded more stereoscopic pictures or larger views in addition to paper portrait photographs. As early as 1863, Charles advertised one of his sets of ambrotype equipment for sale. He apparently had plenty of business by this time, since he was also already advertising for a "good photographic printer" to assist in the gallery.[17]

Charles was not content to sell his views only within Salt Lake City. When he traveled he always tried to arrange to have his pictures sold in the outlying towns, often on consignment, and these contracts spread his work and reputation over a much wider area. Much of his success in these enterprises may be attributed to his reputation for honesty and generosity in his business dealings. Savage's journals are sprinkled with reminders to send copies of views to people who had helped him during his travels.

The Savage family grew steadily. Three more children had been born since leaving New York: Ralph Graham, Annie Amelia, and George Lewis. With four children, a busy studio, and many community and church activities, Charles led an active, full life in Utah and he could easily have sunk into relative obscurity. His love of travel and adventure would not let him rest for long, however. Photographic trips into the wilds of Utah satisfied him for a while, but soon the spirit of wanderlust led him to a much larger adventure.

NOTES

1. Savage Journals, April 30, 1860.
2. Savage Journals, July 19, July 21, August 23, 1860.
3. Savage Journals, June 22, 1860.
4. *Deseret News*, October 10, 1860.
5. For an excellent description of Church trains in the 1860s, see Hulmston.
6. This refers to cattle killed during the guerrilla warfare of the Utah War.
7. Savage Journals, July 28, 1860.
8. Wadsworth, *Through Camera Eyes*, 133.
9. William Clayton to George Q. Cannon, July 16, 1861, in the *Millennial Star*, xxiii (1861) 506.
10. Arrington, 211.
11. Savage Journals, December 22, 23, 1861.
12. Savage Journals, February 27, 1874.
13. Commission papers, signed by Governor Charles Durkee, in Savage Book of Remembrance.
14. Clark, *Life Sketch of Charles Roscoe Savage.*
15. Citizenship papers dated March 16, 1864, in Savage Book of Remembrance.
16. *Deseret News,* December 9, 1863.
17. *Deseret News,* February 18 and October 14, 1863.

CHAPTER 4

A Photographic Tour

AS the year 1866 began, Charles found himself at an impasse. His first ten years in the photographic business had made him a veteran in the use of the collodion wet-plate process, and six of those years in Salt Lake City had established him as a solid businessman. He now usually worked alone, as his partner George Ottinger spent little time in the studio. Since 1863, when Ottinger began painting scenery in the newly completed Salt Lake Theater, Charles had assumed ever greater responsibilities in the partnership. Ottinger became increasingly involved with local theatrical productions as well as scenery painting, and by 1867 had retired from active participation in the firm. He continued to paint scenes of Salt Lake and its environs, which he sold in the gallery, and remained a legal partner until the early 1870s. Eventually the name of the gallery was changed to the Pioneer Art Gallery.

Competition in the photographic field had increased in Salt Lake City, and Savage, always an astute businessman, began to feel that his gallery needed an additional boost. The handcrafted view cameras that had served him so well since the early days in Council Bluffs were showing their age, but the cost of ordering new equipment to be shipped across the plains was prohibitive—the freight costs usually at least doubled the price of any commodity. Savage longed for new equipment to improve the quality of his photographs; in his journal he often lamented the difficulty of working with outdated tools. Although he subscribed to photographic journals and read extensively about advances in the art, he grew impatient with his isolation from progressive photographers with whom he might trade formulas and other information.

After long deliberation, Charles made a decision that affected his career for many years. He planned a grand tour of the major photographic studios in the United States, a tour that would last three months and cover nine thousand miles. This trip would provide him with the opportunity to visit fellow cameramen across the country and learn the latest techniques, as well as the chance to stock up on new equipment for his studio. He also hoped to cultivate relationships with newspapers who might publish reproductions of his photographs, and visit old friends at the same time. This bold plan seemed almost madness for a struggling photographer in the early days of the Old West, but he hoped to make it a financial success by opening new markets for the sale of his photographs and by increasing his photographic skills. In an article later published in *The Philadelphia Photographer*,[1] Savage described many of the details of his trip, and his journal entries provide further information.

In early March, the young photographer boarded an Overland Stage bound for California. He was unimpressed by the scenery that he passed west of Salt Lake City, as he describes in his article:

As one progresses westward, the country becomes more and more uninteresting, culminating in the Desert—a stretch of land of ninety miles, without water, barren, desolate, and God-forsaken, without a blade of

FIGURE 24. (OPPOSITE)
Drawing of the Overland Stage by Overland Stage Company agent A. Stein. Carte-de-visite, 1865. Collection of Carl Mautz.

grass or a green thing of any sort. Water for the use of the stations is conveyed in boxes on wagons, from the nearest spring. The tourist in search of landscapes will find but very few combinations that will make pictures, for the stations are the only objects of particular interest, and a picture of any one of them would be a picture of them all, there is so little difference between them. . . . I do not think it possible to secure more than five or six good views in the distance of four hundred miles west from Salt Lake City.

Despite this dismal conclusion, Charles did find at least one subject worth capturing, if only he had taken a camera!

At Fish Springs I saw about fifteen Indians basking in the sunshine on a heap of manure. It occurred to me that such a group would be interesting to the admirers of the "noble red men of the forest," and if I had been prepared, [I] would have secured a negative of such a "LAY-OUT."

Further west the stage stopped at Austin, one of the boom towns that sprang up in the Nevada Territory to serve the silver-mining industry. Savage disapproved of the wild lifestyle present in these boom towns, but described his visit with his usual mixture of sharp wit and humor:

Austin, Nevada, is located in a narrow canon, and is a fair specimen of what "quartz on the brain" can accomplish in a few years. In all these mining towns we may find the representatives of almost every nation. Here the reformed Shoshone Indian saws wood

and gets gloriously tight. There the China-man does the laundry work, instead of its being done by the ladies, who, by the way, are few and far between in this delightful city, that can neither boast of a garden or a tree. On every hand you hear the clatter clatter of the stamps pulverizing the silver ore, and the hills on each side of the town are honeycombed by the burrowing miner. "Feet," "feet," "feet" is the universal talk.

I found a gentleman of the Teutonic persuasion trying to keep a gallery, sans chemicals, sans books, sans almost everything. It occurred to me that there was a fine chance for a live photographer in that town. I urged the claims of the various photographic publications upon him, and I hope he has profited by the suggestion.

He continued by stage to Placerville and then to Shingle Springs, where he boarded a Central Pacific train to Sacramento. A steamer brought him to the frontier metropolis of San Francisco, where he stayed for a while and made a thorough survey of the photographic studios. His delight in visiting these galleries is evident in his description of San Francisco.

I lost no time in exploring its fine streets and observing its photographic productions. I may say that I was charmed with what I saw. I saw many very fine galleries and spirited go-ahead photographers. Here the porcelain picture is known by the poetic appellation of "Sun Pearls." Every style of work can be obtained equal, with few exceptions, to any work I ever saw. The *Philadelphia Photographer* was in many of the galleries, and much thought of.

While in San Francisco he visited Carleton E. Watkins, who was then perhaps the best known photographer in the western United States. In the early 1860s Watkins was already producing large scenic views in California that were marketed throughout the States and in Europe. Although other photographers such as William Henry Jackson of Omaha, Nebraska, and Eadweard Muybridge of California became famous in the 1870s for their innovative work, at this time Watkins was the premier photographer of the West. Because of his work during the late 1860s, Savage himself would soon rival Watkins in fame as a western scenic photographer. Charles found the California cameraman both helpful and friendly, and his article contains a glowing report of the visit with him:

Among the most advanced in the photographic art, none stands higher than Mr. E. C. Watkins, who has produced, with his camera, results second to none in either the eastern or western hemispheres. I spent many pleasant hours with him, and found him ever ready to communicate information to the ardent photographer.

I was somewhat curious to learn his *modus operandi* for producing his large views in a climate so dry and difficult to work in. After so much attention to photographic ware, porcelain, rubber, and other materials for making baths, I found *his* to consist of pine wood coated heavily with shellac. In addition to this, he uses the water bath, by means of which he can take a greater number of pictures without losing his chances while the light is good. His negatives are taken, developed, and then placed in the water bath until he is ready to finish them. Just think of car-

rying such huge baths, glasses, &c., on muleback, and you can form some idea of the difficulties in the way of producing such magnificent results. . . .

Great quantities of Mr. Watkins' pictures are sold in the Eastern States and Europe, as well as in California. Messrs. Lawrence & Houseworth publish some very fine stereoscopic views, and the galleries of Messrs. Bradley & Rulofson, Shew, Selleck, and many others, are equal in appointments and style of work to those of first-class galleries in the Eastern States.

The firm of Lawrence and Houseworth was one of the major photographic distributors in California in the 1860s and 70s. Starting as an optician's shop, the firm eventually dealt almost exclusively in the manufacture and sale of stereoscopic scenic views. They often purchased negatives or prints from other studios, and sold prints without crediting the original photographer. So widespread was this practice that today it is difficult to identify the original photographer for many of these stereographs.

From San Francisco, Charles boarded the P.M. Company steamship, the "Golden Age," which departed for Panama on March 19. Luckily, his 1866 journal, which is disappointingly blank for most of the year, has a detailed account of this part of his trip. The extra leisure time incident to steamship travel probably accounts for his faithful entries, while the rigor of overland travel explains his lack of entries during those stages of the journey.

The journal account demonstrates the photographer's interest in scientific matters, as he kept a careful daily record of latitude, longitude, miles traveled, temperature, and weather

FIGURE 26.
Artists Virgil Williams and Thomas Hill photographed by Carlton Watkins in Yosemite Valley. Carte-de-visite, c. 1865. Collection of Carl Mautz.

FIGURE 27.
Studio of Lawrence & Houseworth, stereoview, c. 1868.

conditions while on the steamer. His artistic sense is also revealed in his many descriptions of the scenery and of life on board the steamship:

March 22. What a beautiful day. Such calm beautiful weather. On our left can dimly be seen the slopes of the hills of the western shores of lower California. Now and then a blow of a whale or immense flocks of little white birds. In our wake can be seen hundreds of gray and white gulls picking up with the avidity of chickens the refuse of our ship. On the deck are 20 or 30 groups of men, women, and children, playing at every kind of game, what can be imagined to while away the monotony of the day—chess, chequers, cards, dominoes, etc. The lurching and trembling of our ship is not noticed, all with the exception of the very sick have got their sea legs. Our daily fare consists of for breakfast, coffee with milk from cows kept on board the steamer, fish kept on ice, mutton, plus beef with regular tables, fresh bread, and in fact, the usual fare of hotel life on land. Lunch at 12:00 and dinner at 5:00, 5 courses winding up with fruit and pastry.

March 26. Numbers of Mexicans in prettily finished boats came out to take passengers to town about ½ of mile distance. There are also some 20 dugouts containing bananas, pineapple, oranges, shells, limes, coconuts, &c. To the west of the town may be seen the large coal sheds of the Pacific Company and a little further on the graveyard of Europeans that have died in or about the town. A grove of Koco Nut Trees having to the northern eye a very tropical and unusual appearance, immense numbers of

large fish are diving and jumping around the vessel. On the hills are seen the dark green foliage of the orange tree, with other tropical trees looking very pleasant and agreeable. The town looks like an odd mixture of houses in every shape of decay, an old church on the hillside has gone to ruin, and many houses present the same appearance.

During this voyage Savage witnessed part of the battles of the Mexican Revolution from offshore Acapulco, as well as a total eclipse of the moon. He found most of his fellow travelers sociable, although the subject of the Mormon faith came up from time to time, occasionally "with bitter remarks. None of the conclusions the result of a knowledge but of prejudice." He further remarked, "I found myself an object of interest among the ladies, they having found out I was a Mormon. Many a sly whisper and titter at the man of many wives (in their estimation)."[2]

On April 1 the steamship arrived at Panama, where the passengers crossed the isthmus by rail and horse carriage to catch another steamship north to New York. In his article, Savage expresses both his excitement at visiting with Eastern photographic experts and his frustrations with photographing while crossing the plains.

I could not help contrasting the free and liberal manner of the leading photographers, compared with those of ten years ago. At that time, in company with a gentleman, now editor of the *Salt Lake Telegraph*, I took the first stereograph ever taken on Long Island, and on one occasion "got stuck." We applied to a photographer on Broadway to help us out of our difficulty, which he graciously did at the rate of $5.00 per hour for instructions.

FIGURE 28.
Sketch from Savage's 1866 journal entitled "Coal Shed at Acapulco." Collection of Brigham Young University.

If my memory serves me, he did nothing more than rectify the bath, which was foggy, or he may have detected some derangement in the apparatus. Then the intensifier was a profound secret, a collodion formula, one of the hidden mysteries; winks, nods, and secrets prevailed; every operator was a scientific Bluebeard who held the keys of photographic science.

Thank heaven a brighter era has dawned; he who reads may now know everything necessary, combined with practice, to do as well as his neighbor. Noble spirits have ventilated the subject, and given to the world the results of labors for which they will never get recompense, pecuniarily. I am so tired of photographic secrets that I have but a small opinion of men who profess to have them.

Seven years ago photography was found in the upper stories, in garrets, in yards, and other out-of-the-way places; it is now *out to the front*, occupying a very prominent position in the principal business avenues; splendid buildings devoted to heliography now adorn our cities, both in the East and West. I think Philadelphia carries off the palm for the finest plain work, as far as my observation goes, in spite of all of my prejudices in favor of New York. I would not state this much, if it were merely my individual opinion, but it is sustained by half a dozen good critical judges from the West. Fortunately for the reputation of Boston and New York, the barbarians of Utah are not supposed to know much.

One of the objects of my visit eastward was to obtain a wagon suited for taking a series of views on the overland route on my return trip. By Mr. Rech, Girard Avenue, Philadelphia, I had a wagon made suitable for the purpose, and shipped by rail and steamboat to Nebraska City. With the exception of being a little too heavy, it answers pretty well; but like every other thing, it can be improved upon. It is about nine feet long and six feet high in the dark-room, leaving three feet of space in front for carrying a seat and provisions. The sides are filled with grooved drawers, for the different sized negatives, and proper receptacles for the different cameras, chemicals, &c., forming a very complete outdoor darkroom. The principal objection I have to it is, that it will get too hot in the summertime. I propose this year to cover it with white muslin two inches from the outside, so as to keep it cooler; the sides are of sheet-iron, for lightness and to obviate shrinking; the body rests upon the best platform springs.

Provided with Globes, Dallmeyer Triplets, American Optical Company's thirds, chemicals, and everything to suit, I reluctantly left the land of photographic wonders, and followed the *iron horse* to St. Joseph, thence by river to Nebraska City. I did not fail to take a peep at the galleries in the river towns. I am sorry to admit that matters are at a low ebb at most points on the Missouri River. The classical term of *"one-horse-galleries"* will apply to the *palaces of art* on the "Great Muddy." I distributed some of your Journals, and hope they have taken root and borne a hundred-fold. So very few men seem inspired with ambition to do something extra, that the art is almost dormant with them. I scarcely found a room that possessed a View lens; most photographers find such an article a good investment. It is surprising

FIGURE 29.
Engraving of a wet–plate stereo camera.

FIGURE 30.
Engraving of an early stereoviewer.

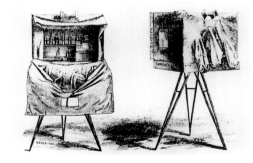

FIGURE 31.
"Carbutt's Portable Developing Box," c. 1865. Wilson and Hood advertised these for $35 each.

that so many do not see it. I found some men that know it all; of course they have stopped learning. I asked one of them how the carbon prints were made? He blandly told me that they were produced by subjecting the sensitized plates to the fumes of carbonic acid gas! Whenever I find a man that has got anything to learn, I know he will be somebody some day.

With two span of mules and provisions for two months, I joined a Mormon train which left Nebraska City for Salt Lake about the 8th of July. As the Mormon trains are all well armed and completely organized, I found it a great advantage, rather than attempt the trip alone, which, by the way, our kind Uncle will not allow any one to do beyond Fort Kearny.[3]

We move slowly the first few days, and gradually increase our pace until we make about twenty-five miles a day. The *modus operandi* of managing a train is as follows: About five o'clock the bugle or reveille is sounded to call up the passengers to prepare their breakfast. About six o'clock all hands are called for prayers; that duty over, preparations are then made to rollout; the caravan then travels until about half past eleven or twelve o'clock, then dinner is prepared, and at two p.m. the journey is resumed, and another camp is made about 6 o'clock. The night-herders then take charge of the herd, and drive them to a good feeding-ground for the night; supper is then prepared, then prayers by the night camp-fires, and the orders for the next day's travel are given by the captain, which winds up the day's journey; guards are then placed around the camp, who are expected to keep a sharp lookout for any sneaking red-skins.

The road from Nebraska City to Fort Kearney presents but few objects of special interest to the photographer. I secured negatives of one or two of the overland stations, and a few rural scenes not remarkable for any particular features different from the genre of subjects elsewhere. When we reached Fort Kearney it was blowing a gale of wind, but, in spite of that, I made a desperate effort to take the Fort, with indifferent success.

From Fort Kearney on to the crossing of the South Platte, near the present terminus of the U.P.R.R., the road follows the Platte Valley, and a more uninteresting road can hardly be found. Very few trees to be seen, and what with the swarms of green flies and mosquitos, and the strong wind that blows regularly every day, your photographic enthusiasm gets cooled down so much that you see nothing worth taking under the circumstances of such a trip. Added to this, you are never free from Indian attacks, for, at the time of our passing along that route, the few settlers on the mail-road were almost scared out of their wits from rumors of Indian troubles.

Now to photograph successfully on the Plains, you must be perfectly safe from Indians, as on two or three occasions in our efforts to secure some views, we found ourselves alone several miles from the train, and ran one or two risks of being gobbled up by a few stray rascals who are always on the lookout for a weak party, and generally manage to pounce down upon a few defenseless wagons that happen to be passing. The sad fate of your former correspondent, Mr.

Glover, shows how uncertain is life in such a place, and the wisdom of keeping a good look-out.[4] The necessary conditions for success under such circumstances are, that you must have plenty of time at your disposal, a strong party well armed with good Henry rifles, and good animals. A company of men could manage to do something. As it was, I did but little, for, on several occasions, when I reached a place of interest, it sometimes blew a gale, or we had a thunder-storm, or it was the middle of the day, and too hot for working; rarely were the circumstances favorable for producing fine views.

We followed the old road after crossing the South Platte at Fremont's Springs, and kept up on the south side of the North Platte; there we found abundance of wild game, such as antelope, deer, prairie fowl, sage hens, &c.; from Ash Hollow on to Laramie the scenery increases in interest, and there are many fine subjects for the camera and pencil. Scott's Bluff, Castle Rock, and Chimney Rock, are fine subjects, and relieve the tedium of the trip considerably. I secured a view of Chimney Rock and Castle Rock, but could not do anything with Scott's Bluff, on account of arriving there in the middle of the day, for our wagon got so hot that we could only work in the morning or in the evening.

After leaving Fort Laramie we strike the Black Hills, and from this point to Salt Lake City we have a succession of scenes of great interest and beauty, if we follow the old emigrant route via the North Platte bridge, Independence Rock, Devil's Gate, and the Sweetwater country, to the South Pass. The last-mentioned point is the dividing ridge for

the whole trip. Here we have a fine view of the Wind River Mountains, clad in eternal snow. West of the Pass we strike Pacific Creek, whose waters, after uniting with the Sandy, flow into Green River, and finally into the Colorado and the Gulf of California. A drive of about one hundred miles brings us to Fort Bridger. From there to Salt Lake City the road winds through canons and valleys, and offers many features of great interest to the tourist photographer.

There is a certain monotony connected with the overland route, and the more one sees of it the less he will admire it. It is in the neighborhood of Salt Lake City that the principal interest of the whole route is centered. The Wahsatch Mountains, the Great Salt Lake, the City and Valley, the Hot Springs, the orchards, gardens, &c., offering such a great contrast to the sterility of one thousand miles that the traveller is lost in astonishment at what he sees. You can readily imagine it was with a feeling of pleasure that we arrived home to the land of apricots, peaches, and every kind of fruit, after the bacon and beans of the Plains, and exchanged the unceasing watchfulness for the quiet and peace of home, for on the Plains no man can feel truly safe at any time.

The reader, by this time, will readily see that photographing in the circumstances under which we travelled, is work; what with the care of animals, and standing guard at nights, and leaving no time to spare, it was a scramble to photograph anything, and unless a man can travel with art companions he can do but little.

To photograph successfully on the Plains and Mountains, you must be well prepared, and, as you will not care to try a view over again after you have once passed the same place, by all means stick to the wet process. After having two or three samples of collodion made expressly for the trip, including an alcoholic collodion, I found the ordinary samples, properly diluted, to do as well as any, and herein lies the principal difficulty, for everything evaporates at a fearful rate, and you must watch your collodion very closely. The cameras of all the makers shrink in this country. The plate-holders went first, fortunately. In New York I saw one made of rosewood that had been in use for two or three years, apparently just as good as new. I took the hint and had some made, and pronounce them the *ne plus ultra* for dry latitudes, as the silver solution does not seem to act upon them at all. I have a pile of ordinary holders all shrunken and useless. The rosewood holders have not changed. The American Optical Company's cameras stand pretty well, but the wood and brass-work do not work well together. They seem the best we have. For baths, I use the solid glass in wooden cases, and for dippers, I prefer those made of whalebone. I used Mr. H. T. Anthony's tanno-gelatine developer, and, on account of its keeping qualities, it is first-rate.

Now, if a dozen photographers and painters will unite in one company, and come to the end of the U.P.R.R., from there get two or three mule-teams with light wagons, and any of your portable tents for photographing, proper negative boxes, and every arrangement complete for packing chemicals (always preparing for an UPSET in crossing the Plains), provisions, and other necessities, a *Ballard*, or a *Henry* rifle to each man;

water-proof coat and blanket; two pair of good boots (one water-proof); one or two good suits of good strong clothes; hams, crackers, yeast powders, dried apples, beans, preserved milk, canned fruits, sardines, and other chemicals, I can promise them as good a time as they ever had in their lives. Prepare to wait one or two days at a point to get good pictures, make up their minds not to be in a hurry, and a series of views can be got that will repay the trouble of producing them. And when they get to the City of Saints, let them call upon Savage and Ottinger, and we will give them the best we have in the shop. Or should any person or persons wish any information about photographing on the Great Plains, it will be cheerfully given by their humble servant, C. R. SAVAGE, Great Salt Lake City, August, 1867.[5]

Charles took a number of photographs during this trip across the plains, despite the difficult conditions. After his return to Salt Lake City, he sent copies of several of these photographs to the editors of *The Philadelphia Photographer* and the *Deseret News*, who listed the pictures by name but could not reproduce them in print, since the photo-mechanical processes for such illustrations had not yet been developed.[6] At least twelve photographs are known to have been taken and later printed, although he may have taken several times that number.[7] It is clear from his article and from accounts in the Salt Lake City newspapers written during his absence that photographing across the Plains was a major objective of the trip. At least six images taken by Savage on this trip have survived in one form or another.[8]

The image shown in figure 34 of a wagon train traveling through Echo Canyon, Utah, has often been attributed to this trip by Savage, but was actually taken by Charles W. Carter, probably the following year.[9] Carter was another English-born Mormon photographer who arrived in Salt Lake City several years after Savage,[10] and worked for Savage and Ottinger for at least a short while, although the exact time and duration of this employment is not known.[11] Some authors have dismissed the idea of Carter's having taken this picture,[12] but the original negative has been identified in a collection of Carter glass-plate negatives.[13] A number of other images from Utah's past have been credited to both Savage and Carter, and it is often difficult to determine which photographer took a given picture. To complicate matters, Carter often made copies of other photographers' work, and apparently printed and sold these images over the years.[14]

Thus concluded Savage's great photographic tour, a trip that significantly altered his life and work. In addition to new equipment and techniques acquired in the East, he returned home with a photographic wagon designed for field work which gave him greater flexibility and freedom to document landscape scenes in the Rocky Mountains. The wagon is shown in a photograph taken on a later trip into the southwest desert areas (fig. 35). With this portable darkroom, he could photograph in areas that would have been inaccessible without this easy means of transporting the cumbersome wet-plate equipment. The wagon, along with the published account of his journey, gave Charles the reputation of a photographer willing to go to any length to obtain fine landscape views.

The photographic wagon was a novelty in Salt Lake City. The local newspapers had

FIGURE 34.
Mormon emigrants in Echo Canyon, Utah, c. 1865. Carte-de-visite by C. W. Carter. Collection of L.D.S. Church Archives.

covered Savage's trip, and on July 5, 1866, proclaimed that he was "on his way from the East." Once home, the paper celebrated his return with an article on August 30 complete with some good-natured teasing about his narrow escapes from Indian attacks. "He crossed the plains," quipped the journalist, "in a very pretty photographic perambulator, taking scenes and views by the way of the Overland Route." The article finished by stating: "Charles, you are welcome back, 'scalps,' plunder, and all."

The possible business applications of the photographic wagon were not ignored. Within a few days of Savage's arrival home, notices appeared in the local papers informing the public that the "Lightning View Wagon" would be available to take pictures of local stores, residences, mines, or other property.[15]

The trip to the East helped Savage's business in other ways, not the least of which was the opening of Eastern markets to the sale of his views. Through contacts made on this trip, Charles began distributing his views for sale, often on commission. With a keen instinct for business, he also made arrangements to become a distributor himself for books, photographs, and other commodities from the East, selling them in his studio. One such arrangement was made with Samuel R. Wells, the proprietor of the New York City firm of Fowler and Wells. Wells was a practitioner of phrenology, the science—or pseudo-science—of interpreting a person's character and personality by examining his head and facial features. Besides selling and publishing books on phrenology, he operated a studio where visitors could see skulls, mummies, casts, and diagrams of the art. After he returned to Salt Lake, Savage sent a photograph of Brigham Young to Wells, who reproduced it as a lithograph in *The Illustrated Annual of Phrenology and Physiognomy for 1866*, with an interpretation of Young's character based on the photograph. Wells gave a great deal of publicity to Savage's studio, in addition to selling photographs and paintings by Savage and Ottinger, and the Utah artists, in turn, became distributors for many of Wells' publications. This association benefited both parties over the years.

Charles also wrote an illustrated booklet entitled *Salt Lake City and the Way Thither*, a travelogue or guidebook for people crossing the Great Plains, illustrated with lithographs made from his photographs. Several issues of this booklet were published by Nelson and Sons and were fairly widely distributed, with Charles retaining the distribution rights in parts of the West. Within a few years of his trip east we find a diary entry (April 12, 1869) stating: "Received a letter from Nelson and Sons granting exclusive agency west of Missouri River for the large view of the city and the smaller book. They wanted to claim San Frisco, but I declined, giving them Texas, St. Louis, Missouri, Kansas in exchange." Other similar guidebooks and pictorial books followed over the years. Some of Savage's pictures were also used in travel guides by other authors published during this era.[16]

Although not specifically mentioned in his sparse journal entries of the 1860s, Charles appears to have been friends with Edward L. Wilson, editor of *The Philadelphia Photographer*,

even before his trip east.[17] He had contributed several letters to the journal prior to this time, including photographs sent to them for review.[18] While in Philadelphia he undoubtedly visited Wilson, who was an influential leader of the photographic community. The account of Savage's journey in *The Philadelphia Photographer* gave him a great deal of publicity, and doubtless helped open the eastern markets to later sale of his photographs. In turn, Savage and Ottinger's Gallery retailed *The Philadelphia Photographer* for many years.

Charles had also contributed letters to *Humphrey's Journal of Photography and the Allied Arts and Sciences*. These letters often included sample photographs by Savage, and in one case a new formula for collodion, while another letter described the "Lime and Gold Toning Bath."[19] Despite his relative isolation in frontier Utah, the young photographer had clearly kept up his contacts in the East. These friendships were renewed and strengthened on the photographic tour.

His new friends on the West Coast proved a great boon as well. Carleton E. Watkins of San Francisco remained a lifelong friend. In later years, when Watkins became the official photographer of the Central Pacific Railroad, his influence was probably behind the official assistance given to Savage in photographing along the railroad routes.

Savage also developed an affiliation with the prominent newspaper, *Harper's Weekly*. The exact nature of these arrangements is uncertain, but Savage left some photographs with the editors of the paper during his stay in New York.[20] The August 18, 1866, issue of *Harper's* published an article entitled "City and Valley of the Great Salt Lake," a glowing account of

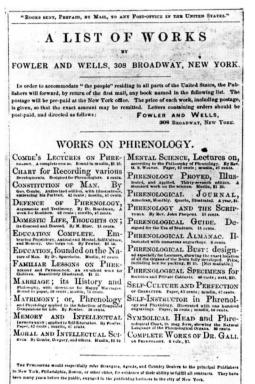

FIGURE 36.
Advertisements for phrenology books offered by Fowler & Wells. From Savage's Scrapbook, Brigham Young University.

FIGURE 37.
Centerfold of Harper's Weekly, *August 18, 1866,*
illustrated with wood engravings from Savage views.
Collection of L.D.S. Historical Department.

Salt Lake City, extolling its newer buildings, progressive school system, and agricultural delights. It was illustrated with lithographs made from Savage photos, including a panorama of Salt Lake City, the Tabernacle under construction, the Beehive House, the Salt Lake Theater, the tithing office, and the old Tabernacle. Also included were individual portraits of Brigham Young and the Twelve Apostles. Whether Charles wrote the entire piece or only supplied the essential information is unknown. However, the final paragraph of the article demonstrates both admiration for the Utah residents and a decidedly Mormon tone, making it likely to have come from his hand:

We cannot close this notice without adding that with whatever differences of opinion may be entertained of the Mormon faith, the great virtue of labor cannot be denied to the Mormon population; and high admiration is universally expressed of the executive ability of Brigham Young, who has redeemed the wilderness, made it a fruitful field, and "made the desert to blossom as a rose."

After his arrival home, Charles sent copies of some photos taken on the overland trip to *Harper's Weekly*. These, too, were printed as lithograph prints, and began a tradition of publication in *Harper's* that continued for many years. It is unknown whether Savage received any payment from *Harper's*, but in any case, this national exposure placed his photographs before the eyes of the public, and expanded his reputation as a western scenic photographer.[21]

The Anthony brothers of E. and H. T. Anthony Co. in New York may also have been friends of Savage's prior to his trip to the East,[22] possibly from his days in New York City in the late 1850s. Anthony's was at that time the largest photographic supply house in the world, and when Savage needed to stock his photographic wagon he turned to this firm for help. He signed a note for the supplies that totaled $3,400, a large sum at a time when stereo pictures sold for $2.00 a dozen. On the trip home across the Plains, the new photographic wagon evidently tipped over while crossing the Platte River, and a good portion of the supplies were water-damaged or lost in the current. He made only the briefest mention in his article of the incident, advising photographic travelers to pack their chemicals carefully, "always preparing for an UPSET in crossing the Plains." In a later diary entry (February 12, 1879), he explained his loss further, along with the financial difficulties it caused:

In 1870 I foolishly shouldered a debt of $3,400 owing by Savage and Ottinger for goods bought in 1866. Most of said goods being lost in the Platte River and the depre-ciation in value of goods by the railroads entering our valley—business being nearly gone, we dissolved. I shouldered the debt and set George free. I steadily paid on the accepted notes until 1875—possibly $2,600 on three notes at $700 interest. Being again nearly bankrupt, I put off the payment of the remaining notes—hoping as they were out-lawed the parties would offer me a chance of paying them at a reduction of say fifty cents on the dollar—but they never seemed willing to rebate one cent. On the contrary, sued.

This dispute over payment of the note led to bitter feelings between the parties. On an 1878 trip to New York, Charles tried to settle the conflict out of court, noting that "Henry Anthony was quite cordial, but Wilcox and Ed Anthony were not very friendly."[23] Charles struggled with this debt through nearly two decades and several court battles before finally settling with the Anthonys.[24] This debt must have been a bitter pill to swallow for the frugal, self-sufficient Englishman.

In the late 1860s, Savage's fame as a landscape photographer continued to spread. Although portrait photography supplied most of his income, he supplemented it by retailing books, stationary, and landscape and city views. He continued to be a strong supporter of local artists and craftsmen, and his studio was well known as a cultural center, where theater tickets, art supplies, and locally produced artwork could be obtained. The studio was often a meeting point for group excursions or public service groups, and visitors to the city were usually sent to Savage and Ottinger's for picture souvenirs. In addition, his landscape views began to be sold nationwide.

In the May 1868 issue of *The American Phrenological Journal*, edited by Samuel R. Wells, a picture of the Savage and Ottinger studio was published (figures 38), with the following statement:

The above engraving represents the book store and photographic art emporium of Messrs. Savage and Ottinger, in Salt Lake City, Utah Territory. Besides supplying the "Saints" and the "Gentiles" with the best literature of the Old World and the New, they produce good pictures—we may safely say some of the best we have ever seen. Portraits of the "saints" and "sinners," . . . Indians, pictures of trees, mountains, water-falls . . . and some of the most sublime scenery in the world.

These gentlemen are artists! They combine business with art, and supply school books, phrenological books, and every variety of *useful* books.

. . . Here is a store, . . . three thousand miles west from New York, in the center of a vast Territory teeming with life, enterprise, education, and Mormonism! A hundred thousand hardy people now have their homes in these mountains; . . . Look now on one of its first book stores.

George Ottinger also gained in renown during this period. Several paintings were sent by Ottinger to Wells in New York, including a picture of City Creek Falls. This oil painting was sold in 1868 to none other than Schuyler Colfax, who was elected vice-president of the United States the same year. In a letter regarding this painting,[25] Ottinger expressed his gratitude to Wells.

Salt Lake City, Utah   Nov. 6, 1868
Mr. Wells
Dear Sir,

Your letter of the 22d ult recd and I assure you it is no small gratification to me to hear you are so well pleased with the picture. Not only a gratification & satisfaction to feel that so small a gift has been appreciated & accepted in return for the many many kindnesses you have extended to S. & O. but it is also with no little satisfaction I hear that yourself & friends have discovered some merit in my work, enough indeed to place it among your other gems. Now Mr. Wells the only part of the business I'm not satisfied with is your placing $50 to our credit. *We will not stand that.* We have been more than doubly paid for that picture. It is a free gift fresh from the hearts of the givers as a slight token of their esteem and friendship, and as such you must accept it. We will not have it otherwise.

In a few days I shall send you another Canon View as good as the one you have. I send it to you to sell for us and if successful I shall send you more and allow any commission you think proper.

A few months later, Wells devoted several columns of the March 1869 issue of the *American Phrenological Journal* to Ottinger, "The Utah Artist." This article contained a portrait of Ottinger as well as biographical information and a flattering phrenological evaluation.

As the 1860s rushed to their completion, so, too, did the Transcontinental Railroad. Charles Savage was soon to find himself involved in an enterprise of great historical significance, and would take some of the most famous photographs in the history of the West.

NOTES

1. Savage, "A Photographic Tour," 287-289, 313-316.
2. Savage Journals, March 29, March 30, 1866.
3. The U.S. government permitted only fully armed and organized trains to travel west across the frontier. This policy, enforced by the cavalry, was instituted in order to avoid unnecessary loss of life from Indian attack.
4. Ridgeway Glover was an itinerant photographer who traveled west in 1866 to photograph the frontier. He sent three letters east which were published in *The Philadelphia Photographer*. The November 1866 issue of *The Philadelphia Photographer* contained a notice that Glover had been killed by Indians while photographing alone near Fort Phillip Kearney, Nebraska Territory.
5. In *Photography and the American Scene*, Taft notes that this date (1867) is a typographical error. The article was published in January, 1867, and Savage's journals also record that he took this trip in 1866.
6. *The Philadelphia Photographer*, January, 1867, 32; *The Deseret News*, August 30, 1867.
7. The names of the photographs known to have been taken on this trip are from several sources. Three pictures were listed as having been taken in *The Philadelphia Photographer* article. Two related news items, *The Philadelphia Photographer*, January, 1867, 32, and the *Deseret News*, August 30, 1867, give lists of pictures received from Savage after this trip. The partial list of photographs includes: "A Mormon camp, preparing to start across the plains," "A camp of immigrants at Wyoming" [Nebraska] (perhaps the same photo), "A home in Nebraska," "O'Fallon's Bluff, S. Platte," "Farm Scene on Steven's Creek, Nebraska," "Devil's Gate," "Sweetwater," and "Castle Rock N. Platte." The four known extant images complete the total. (see note 8 below).
8. Existing photographic prints include: "Roland Reed Homestead," Nebraska State Historical Society (NSHS) #d3751; "Mormon Train fording S. Platte," NSHS #E54-32; "Mormon Camp, Wyoming, Nebraska," NSHS #E54-31; Road Ranch at Cheese Creek, Nebraska, NSHS #R629-3; and "Pioneers on the plains," L.D.S. Historical Archives #P1069. Two other images from this trip were reproduced as lithographs in *Harper's Weekly*, November 2, 1867 (Cheese Creek photo and a picture of Chimney Rock on the North Platte River).
9. Wadsworth, "Zion's Cameramen."
10. For more information on the career of Charles W. Carter, see Wadsworth, *Through Camera Eyes*.
11. Savage Journals, May 30, 1869. The connection with Savage must have been sometime between November 1864, when Carter arrived in Salt Lake, and 1867, when we find him in his own studio with J. B. Silvis, another photogra-

pher. Since the first Salt Lake City directory published in 1867 listed "C. W. Carter, Photographer, at Savage and Ottinger, res. 6th Ward, n.s. 4th So. between 4th and 5th W.," it is probable that Carter started his own business some time during 1867.
12. Carter, 63.
13. C. W. Carter negative collection, L.D.S. Church Historical Department, access number 118811-ARCH-88, call number PH 1300. Assistance with information about Carter and his photographers was obtained from Jennifer Lund, 536 W. Germania Ave., Murray, UT 84123. Mrs. Lund, a great-granddaughter of Carter, is a researcher and biographer of Carter.
14. A number of copy negatives may be found in the C. W. Carter negative collection.
15. *Salt Lake Daily Telegraph*, September 2, 1866; *Salt Lake Herald*, May 5, 1871.
16. See Crofutt. Engravings in this guide were taken from photographs by Savage, Watkins, and Houseworth.
17. Wilson, 32.
18. "Editor's Table," *The Philadelphia Photographer*, 2:21 (September 1865), 154; and 2:24 (December 1865), 207.
19. "To Correspondents: C. R. Savage," July 15, 1865, 95, and June 1, 1864, 45.
20. That the pictures were left with *Harper's Weekly* prior to his return to Utah is evidenced by the date of publication, August 18. Since he returned home in early August, the pictures could not have been sent back across the plains and prepared for publication in the two weeks or less between his arrival home and August 18.
21. As early as 1862, a Savage picture had been printed in the *Illustrated London News*, the original illustrated weekly that was the model for the U. S. weeklies. It is not known whether Savage sent this picture to England for publication, or whether someone else bought it from him and gave it to the paper.
22. In "A Photographic Tour," Savage referred to H. T. Anthony as "my esteemed friend."
23. Savage Journals, November 6, 1878.
24. The Anthony Brothers initially filed suit in the Third District Court in Salt Lake City, winning their case. Savage appealed to the Supreme Court of the Utah Territory, and the judgment was reversed, but the Anthonys pressed for a new trial. The case dragged on until Savage finally settled in 1883.
25. Original in the Fowler Family Papers.

FIGURE 39.
George M. Ottinger in his military uniform, c. 1875. Collection of the Utah State Historical Society.

CHAPTER 5

Photographer at Promontory

FOR more than three decades the idea of a transcontinental railroad had been espoused by American journalists and statesmen. As the stream of immigrants pushed the frontiers ever further westward, the new settlers were separated from the rest of the nation by hundreds of miles of sparsely inhabited land. Only an occasional mail delivery and common customs served to connect the frontier communities with the eastern cities. California and Oregon were also quickly becoming more populated, and the colonists in these coastal territories felt even more estranged from the United States than did the midwest frontier towns.

These outlying communities were strong advocates of a "Pacific Railroad" to connect the two coasts, not only for the cultural advantages but for economic reasons as well. The rich farmland of the Midwest produced far more crops than could be locally consumed, and the settlers longed for an economical system to transport their produce to eastern markets. A transcontinental railway would also lower the prices of eastern commodities flowing to the frontier, in addition to opening the rich mineral deposits of the West to exploitation.

A variety of other arguments were advanced in support of the railway. What if the rich coastal territories of the West decided to leave the Union, some argued? Alternatively, if California were attacked by a foreign power (Great Britain was the usual scapegoat) how could the United States defend its territory? Military leaders saw the Pacific Railway as a means of suppressing Indian uprisings and, in the aftermath of the Utah War of 1859, of controlling the Mormon settlements as well. Eastern merchants saw the railway as a "gateway to the riches of the Orient," which would allow them to bypass the long and hazardous sea route around Cape Horn. So many and so convincing were the arguments that by the 1860s the only remaining questions were how and where the railroad would be built.

As a result of the Pacific Railroad Surveys of 1853-55, three possible routes for the transcontinental railroad were proposed, and few at that time really believed that more than one railway would ever be completed. The city that served as the eastern railhead for the project would reap tremendous economic benefits, and the advantages of the various routes were hotly debated in the press. With the outbreak of the Civil War in 1861, support vanished for any but the northern route, and Omaha, Nebraska Territory, became the railhead city. In 1862, Congress passed the Railroad Act, which, with its amendments in 1864, provided financial incentives for the railroad companies to begin construction. The Union Pacific Railroad crews began working westward from Omaha in 1864, nearly a year after construction had begun on the Central Pacific Railroad in Sacramento, California. The Union Pacific Railroad and Central Pacific Railroad, although ultimately financed by land grants and subsidies from the federal government, had to provide their own short-term financing to build the railroad. Since both railroads were to receive eventual

FIGURE 40. (OPPOSITE)
Meeting of the locomotives at Promontory. Carte-de-visite by C. R. Savage, 1869. Collection of Harold B. Lee Library, Brigham Young University.

compensation based on the number of miles of track laid, there was fierce competition to press forward with construction, and innovative (and sometimes questionable) methods of raising the necessary capital were used.

The progress of the railroad construction was eagerly followed both in the newspapers and in the files of parlor stereoscopes. A number of photographers traveled westward to document the frontier towns, Indian tribes, and wild country only recently made accessible by the railway. Even in the early stages of construction, photographers were called on to provide publicity and boost financial support for the venture. In the fall of 1866, a publicity event was sponsored by Union Pacific when their track layers crossed the one hundredth meridian of longitude, 247 miles west of Omaha. During a three-day trip, eastern businessmen, politicians, and journalists were entertained in royal fashion aboard plush railroad cars. Activities during the trip included buffalo hunting, staged Indian raids, and sumptuous meals. On the evening of the trip home, a prairie fire was intentionally set to provide a final scenic view for the guests. John Carbutt, a Chicago photographer, was hired to document the trip and to provide photographic mementos for the participants.[1] These photos were later sold to the public, providing further publicity for the railroad. Although a number of later photographers were associated with Union Pacific,[2] Carbutt is the only one documented to have been on its payroll.[3]

This expedition with the railroad was only a temporary position for Carbutt, who later gained prominence in Philadelphia as a developer and manufacturer of the new dry-plate process of photography. He was also an early advocate of the photo-mechanical printing pro-

cesses that revolutionized book illustrations, and a pioneer in medical x-ray photograph technology. He died in 1905 as a result of exposure to x-rays during these experiments.[4]

The success of the 100th Meridian Excursion probably played a significant role in the decision of Union Pacific directors to continue photographic coverage of the construction. The man who eventually photographed most of the Union Pacific Railroad construction was Captain Andrew J. Russell, who began his career as a sign painter and decorator in Nunda, New York. (fig. 41) He worked for a while as a handwriting teacher, and later opened a studio where he painted dioramas and landscapes. He served as a captain in the Union Army in the Civil War,[5] where he was taught photography and assigned as photographer to the U.S. Military Railroad Construction Corps under General Herman Haupt. Russell was the only commissioned military photographer during the Civil War, and he documented railroad operations in Virginia that were crucial to military strategy. Civilian cameramen provided the other principal photo-documentation of the war. Many of these civilian photographers operated under the direction of Matthew Brady, the New York photographer who eventually assumed credit for most of the wartime pictures. Most of Russell's Civil War photographs, including the famous picture of the Rebel dead behind the stone wall at Fredericksburg, were acquired by Brady after the war.

In the spring of 1868, four years after work began in Omaha, Russell began to photo-document the construction of the Union Pacific Railroad. He accompanied the work crews as far west as Weber Canyon, Utah, and photographed the Mormon grading teams working in Weber

Canyon. While there, he took a trip to Salt Lake City, where he met Charles Savage for the first time. Although professional competitors, the photographers seem to have become friends during this period. These educated, intelligent men, upon finding a fellow artist on the frontier, would quite likely have established working and social relationships. At least one of Russell's photographs of Salt Lake City was taken from the roof of the old Council House, next door to Savage's photographic studio,[6] and Charles also spent some time in Weber and Echo canyons photographing the grading and tunnel construction by Mormon teams in the fall of 1868. Many of Savage's images are nearly identical to those taken by Russell, and were clearly taken within a few minutes of Russell's.[7] A photograph taken by Russell in Echo, Utah, probably in the fall of 1868 (fig. 42), shows Russell's photographic wagon, and the man holding the glass plate in the center is Savage.[8] Several other photographs taken at Weber and Echo canyons by Savage show Russell's photographic wagon in the background, and are nearly identical to known Russell photographs.[9]

When work on the railroad slowed for the winter in late 1868, Russell returned to New York and published his first series of stereo views under the Union Pacific label. He also obtained a new, larger stereo camera that he used along with his large format (10" x 13") view camera.[10] Russell's success in producing photographs of brilliant clarity and sharpness was due not only to his great skill as a technician, but also to his use of large formats. His images are beautiful specimens of frontier railroad photography.

The Central Pacific railroad also had its official photographer, Alfred A. Hart, originally from Norwich, Connecticut. (fig. 43). Like Russell, Hart began his career in portrait painting and later moved into photography, probably out of financial necessity.[11] Beginning in 1864, Hart took stereoscopic views of the Central Pacific construction route that were used in newspaper articles as well as sold to the public. He photographed almost entirely in the stereo format, as did many landscape photographers of the day, since most of their income was generated from the sale of cards for parlor stereoscopes. Since Hart was not exclusively employed by the Central Pacific, he sold many of his negatives to the San Francisco firm of Lawrence and Houseworth, which published them under its own label. He also sold stereo views under his own name.[12]

Savage used a number of camera formats, including several large-view formats. Stereo cameras were smaller and more portable, however, and stereo photos had a larger market, so Savage usually took field photographs in the stereo format. The decision by Savage and Hart to use smaller formats for railroad photography limited the scope and clarity of their photographs as compared to those of Russell, although their talents in composition were certainly equal to his. In addition, the only surviving examples of Hart and Savage photos are original albumen prints, which have faded and yellowed over the years, while many of Russell's original negatives still survive, and very sharp, clear prints can be made from them. All three cameramen were veterans of field photography using the wet-plate process.

In 1867, as construction neared Utah and competition between the railroads increased in intensity, both companies courted the Mormon settlers in Utah to assist in the grading. Help from the Mormons was crucial, since they were the only major source of manpower and wagon

FIGURE 43.
Photograph of Alfred A. Hart, c. 1867.
Courtesy of Glenn Williamsen.

teams in the inter-mountain area, and could easily boost the productivity of the railroad they assisted. As part of the efforts to win Brigham Young's support, Central Pacific official Edwin Crocker sent a full set of stereo views to the Mormon prophet, and reported that "he was highly pleased with them." Similar tactics were used by the Union Pacific, for Crocker further stated that Brigham Young "had some from the Union Pacific, but they did not compare to ours."[13] Despite the photographs, the Mormons under the direction of Brigham Young split their support between the railroads.

This contracting with both railroads allowed many L.D.S. immigrants to supplement their agricultural incomes by working for an hourly wage. Much of the tunnel and grading work performed in Weber Canyon was done by Latter-day Saint farmers. Brigham Young was careful to keep the Mormon settlers unified into a single group of laborers, thereby insuring that wages remained high. A number of sermons were preached reminding the Saints that competition between church members would only lower the wages for all. Similar unified fronts were also maintained in the contracts to supply timber, produce, and other commodities to the railroad companies.

The railroad was viewed by the Utah pioneers with a mixture of anticipation and apprehension. Having lived in the valleys of the Rocky Mountains in relative isolation for twenty years, an entire generation of Latter-day Saints had grown up in a tightly knit economic and cultural group. The intervening two decades had not erased the memories of persecution in Missouri and Illinois. The strongly unified Mormons had flourished in the wilderness by following their religion's creed of self-reliance,

hard work, and independence from outside groups. The arrival of the railroad threatened to end this isolation. Many feared that the influx of cheap agricultural and consumer products would deplete Utah of its limited cash reserves and put local merchants and farmers out of work. The arrival of miners to exploit Utah's rich mineral resources was expected to topple the political stability of Mormon society. Those who had long opposed the Latter-day Saint religion felt sure that the resulting political chaos would allow the "oppressed victims of Mormondom" to escape the "strangle-hold" of the church. So widely held was the belief that the railroad would cause the death of "Mormonism" that the national anti-polygamy legislation of the 1860s was temporarily abandoned in the hope that it would no longer be necessary.

The Latter-day Saints also worried about the cultural effects of the railroad on their society. One prominent church member declared:

You can form some estimate of what the results would be to our cities and settlements of 5,000 or 6,000 Irish, German and other laborers crowding through our peaceful vales. It is not the men actually working on the line that I should fear so much, although no doubt they would cause some trouble, and raise a muss occasionally, but it would be the bummers, gamblers, saloon and hurdy-gurdy keepers, border ruffians, and desperadoes generally, who prey upon the laborers, whom I should fear most.

Better . . . for the Saints to do the work for nothing, if necessary, than to let outsiders do it, as it would cost us more to preserve our cattle and horses from thieves, and our families from insult, than to roll up our sleeves and go and do the work ourselves.[14]

The contracts with the railroads for grading and tunnel construction were, in part, intended to limit exposure to the railroad construction crews as well as to boost the local economy. Other steps were taken by church leaders to combat the coming economic crisis. Cooperative enterprises such as the Provo Woolen Mills, Utah Manufacturing Company, and the silk industry were strengthened. Church members were encouraged to deal only with Latter-day Saint merchants and suppliers, and to buy Utah-produced items whenever possible. The Zions Cooperative Mercantile Institution (ZCMI) was organized in October 1868. This central clearing house bought imported materials in volume for distribution to the retail outlets in the Mormon colonies, helping to limit the cash leaving the Territory. The "Word of Wisdom," a health code that encouraged abstinence from tea, coffee, tobacco, and alcohol, was strongly emphasized. The money saved from not importing these commodities was allocated to the Perpetual Emigration Fund to bring more

FIGURE 44.
Mormon workers commencing construction of a railroad tunnel, c. 1868. From a stereoview by C. R. Savage. Collection of the L.D.S. Church Archives.

FIGURE 45.
Tracks near Promontory, 1869. From stereoview by C. R. Savage. Collection of Barry Swackhamer.

FIGURE 46.
Union Pacific locomotive, Jupiter, at Promontory c. 1869. From stereoview by C. R. Savage. Collection of Bill Lee.

FIGURE 47.
Crowd gathered at Promontory, 1869. Carte-de-visite by C. R. Savage. Collection of Harold B. Lee Library, Brigham Young University.

immigrants to Utah on the train, thereby bolstering the local political base.

The economic policy crisis of 1868-69 prompted the emergence of the "New Movement." This group, later named the "Godbeites" after their leader, shop-owner William Godbe, was comprised of talented, intellectual liberals such as E. L. T. Harrison, Edward W. Tullidge, W. H. Shearman, and Eli B. Kelsey. These men campaigned for cooperation with outside parties to develop local mining interests and thus absorb Utah's economy into the national free-trade economy. The Godbeites began *The Utah Magazine*, which ran a series of editorials criticizing the L.D.S. Church policy of discouraging mining and outside trade. This group intended to provide progressive solutions to the economic crisis, but because of open criticism of church policy, Harrison, Godbe, and others of the liberal movement were eventually excommunicated. T. B. H. Stenhouse, Savage's old friend from England, was among the excommunicants.

Charles Savage, although close friends with many of these intelligent, talented men, strongly disapproved of their political stance. When Samuel Wells wrote a series of articles in his phrenological journal praising the "New Movement," Savage sent him a letter that stated, in part:

I notice you give prominence to some of the so-called reformers of Utah—Heaven save the mark. What the Communists were to Paris, so would the New Movers be to Utah. They the Reformers would pull down and destroy what has taken 22 years to build up . . .

I think. Bro. Wells, you ought to go slow in lending your paper too much to the inter-ests of the so-called liberal party—did you live here you wuold pronounce them unmitigated tyrants . . .

I do not say there are not some good men amongst them, but they are very few. [The] Cooperation that they please to style an oligarchy is a great success and a godsend to the people.[15]

Charles was also a strong advocate of buying only locally produced items, and often stated in his advertisements the virtues of Utah products. He wrote articles for the newspaper promoting this same idea, and was a great supporter of local artists and tradesmen.

The protective economic institutions established by the L.D.S. Church did much to prevent or slow the complete absorption of Utah into the free-trade economy, disappointing those who had hoped that Utah would become a "colony" to provide raw materials to the industrial East. Polygamy, as well as the political unity of the Mormons, remained strong, much to the dismay of those who had predicted the downfall of both institutions based on the false assumption that these practices were maintained by force rather than choice. And, despite the cultural shock of the coming of the railroad, the Mormon settlers held fast to their religious teachings, maintaining a spiritual separation from the rest of the world that persists even today.

As the eastern and western railroad teams worked feverishly into the spring of 1869, preparations for the final ceremonies at Promontory Summit were made. Each side knew that it was making history, and planned on making the most of it. Cars of dignitaries and newspaper reporters came from both coasts, and Ogden and Salt Lake City sent their own officials to attend. Alfred Hart and Andrew Russell arranged to be present to photograph the event. Three weeks prior to the "Last Spike" ceremonies, Dan Casement, one of the pair of brothers who managed the Union Pacific work crews, along with other Union Pacific officials, visited the Savage studio.[16] They must have been favorably impressed with his work, for a few days later he was officially invited by Col. Silas Seymour of the Union Pacific to photograph the proceedings at Promontory.[17]

The reason for this invitation is unclear, as Russell had already proven himself equal to the task. The railroad officials may have wished to win the support of Utahns by having a local photographer participate, or they may have known of Savage's national reputation and connections with eastern papers, and wished to capitalize on it. It may even have been a case of one-upmanship—the Union Pacific would have two photographers to Central Pacific's one. Given the national significance of the event, it is surprising that only three photographers were present. Several photographers lived in the Salt Lake area during this period, including Charles Carter, who was actively involved in field photography. A number of photographers traveled west on the railroad to take pictures shortly after completion of the line. One of these later photographers, William Henry Jackson, was married that weekend,[18] but given the wide publicity and the number of newspaper reporters present, other photographers might have been expected to attend. In any case, the presence of these three photographers provided a question that would puzzle historians for many years: who photographed what at Promontory Summit?

Charles left Salt Lake City on the Wells Fargo coach on May 6, on his way to Promontory. He arrived at Taylor's Mill (presently Riverdale) and spent the night in the ticket agent's office. The following morning he caught a ride on a Union Pacific train out to the Casement camp near Promontory Summit. Here he was informed that the ceremonies scheduled for the next day would be delayed until Monday, May 10. Spring rains had washed out a trestle in Weber Canyon, causing a two-day delay for the Union Pacific delegation while the trestle was repaired and tested. This forty-eight-hour delay was fortuitous from a historical perspective, since the rain would also have made photography much more difficult. Savage spent the time exploring the area, and "took 3 or 4 negatives around Casement's camp."[19] Figure 48, entitled "Casement's men going to work," may be one of these photographs.[20] It depicts part of Jack Casement's team of Irish tracklayers on a flat-car next to Union Pacific Engine No. 66. It is difficult to date this stereograph precisely, and it could also have been taken during the fall of 1868 when Savage was photographing further eastward along the Union Pacific line.[21]

In addition to meeting Russell and Hart on May 7, Charles sold a number of photographic prints to the railroad men and the Central Pacific delegation. He even complained of some views being "stolen by the democrats" (presumably the construction crews). He further recorded in his journal that day the rough life led by the railroad workers:

In sight of their camp were the beautiful city of [D]eadfall and [L]ast [C]hance. I was creditably informed that 24 men had been killed in the several camps in the last 25 days. Certainly a harder set of men were never before congregated together before. The

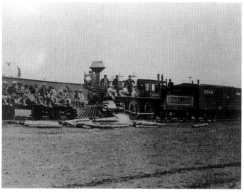

FIGURE 48.
Jack Casement's Irish workmen going to work on the line of the Union Pacific Railroad. From stereoview by C. R. Savage, c. 1868-69. Collection of Barry Swackhamer.

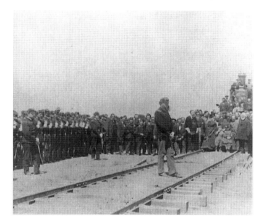

FIGURE 49.
Military officers at the laying of the last rail. From stereoview by C. R. Savage, 1869. Collection of James P. Crain.

FIGURE 50.
Ceremony to join the rails at Promontory, 1869. View by A. J. Russell. Original negative in the collection of the Oakland Museum.

FIGURE 51.
Ceremony to join the rails at Promontory, 1869. Carte-de-visite by C. R. Savage. Collection of Carl Mautz.

FIGURE 52.
Crowd gathered at the ceremony to join the rails at Promontory, 1869. Carte-de-visite by C. R. Savage. Collection of Carl Mautz.

company do the country a service in sending such men back to Omaha, for their presence would be a scourge upon any community. At Blue River the returning demons . . . were being piled upon the cars in every stage of drunkenness. Every ranch or tent has whiskey for sale. Verily the men earn their money like horses and spend it like asses.

On Sunday, May 9, Savage went to Promontory which, he said, "consists of ½ doz. tents and Rum holes; is 9 miles from water."[22] The next day dawned clear and cool; beautiful weather for dignitaries and cameramen alike. The Central Pacific delegation arrived first, pulled in by the locomotive, "Jupiter."

Once the Union Pacific delegation arrived with its engine No. 119, the two locomotives moved forward until only one length of rail separated them. The last tie, a polished laurel tie presented by a California firm, was placed into position. Jack Casement's crack team of Irish track-layers carried one rail forward for the Union Pacific, with the Central Pacific rail being placed by a team of Chinese workers. As this rail was brought forward, someone in the crowd shouted to Savage: "Now's the time, Charlie, take a shot!" The Chinese laborers, unfamiliar with cameras and sure that their lives were in danger, dropped the rail and scattered wildly, to the laughter of the crowd. Only after much coaxing were they convinced to return and lay the rail in the proper position.[23]

Speeches and prayers were next offered, and the photographers took several pictures of the group surrounding the last tie. Most of these pictures seem carefully posed, and the images produced by the different photographers are very similar.

After the speeches, the gold and silver spikes were dropped into pre-drilled holes in the laurel tie, and the last two iron spikes were driven by Leland Stanford for the Central Pacific and Thomas Durant for the Union Pacific. An observer of the ceremonies stated that only one photograph of the actual driving of the last spike was taken, and the glass plate was broken in the confusion of the celebration following the ceremony.[24] Confusion there was, for immediately after the laurel tie was removed and replaced by a regular tie and iron spikes, the crowd rushed forward with knives and completely destroyed the tie by cutting pieces off for souvenirs. Six ties were planted in turn before the crowd would leave one in place.[25] This probably accounts, in part, for the multitude of iron spikes "discovered" in later years, each with a claim of being the last spike.

The two engines inched forward across the new rails until they touched, and at that point Russell and Savage took their classic pictures of the engines meeting at Promontory. Russell's photo, entitled "East meets West at the laying of the last rail" (fig. 50), shows the two engines together with chief engineers Grenville Dodge of Union Pacific and Samuel Montague of Central Pacific shaking hands, and the rest of the crowd stretched out in a beautifully composed "V". Savage's two images of "Meeting of Locomotives at Promontory" (fig. 40 and 51) are very similar to Russell's picture, although enough differences exist to make comparisons. All three photographs use the compelling imagery of two engines meeting on the final track, each from the opposite side of the nation. Figure 40 is the Savage view most often reproduced, and errors have understandably been made in mistaking this image for Russell's "East meets West" photo-

FIGURE 53.
Wood engraving from June 5, 1869, issue of
Harper's Weekly *depicting the "Joining of the Rails"*
celebration at Promontory.

graph. The photographs show that the two cameramen were standing within a few feet of each
other, and the camera in the foreground of Savage's view may actually be Russell's camera. At
least four of Savage's photos at Promontory were
taken in the stereo format, although he later
printed both stereo and carte-de-visite prints
from the same negative.[26] It is reasonable to
assume that many, if not all, of his other Promontory pictures were also originally taken as
stereo negatives. Savage himself described his day
at Promontory in the following terms:

> Today the ceremony of linking the ends
> of the tracks took place. I worked . . . all day
> and secured some nice views of the scenes
> connected with laying the last rail—Was
> informed by Bishop Sharp that my name

had been included in Salt Lake Delegation to
the officer of the roads. Everything passed
of[f] lively and the weather was delightful.
Saw but little of the actual driving of the gold
spike and laying of the laurel tie as I was very
busy—Left the promontory . . . and reached
Ogden at 10:00. Cracked champagne with
Brother Jennings and others at West's Hotel,
where I stayed for the night.[27]

At least ten or eleven photographs were
taken by Charles in and around Promontory,
but only eight images are known by the author
to exist today.[28] It is very possible that other Savage images of Promontory are hidden away in
private collections or museum archives.

Within a few days of the Last Spike celebration, Charles sent "copies of each kind" of

Promontory view to *Harper's Weekly*.[29] It is not known whether he was requested by the paper to send these pictures, but given the relatively short notice Savage had in preparing for his trip to Promontory, it is unlikely. The pictures were probably submitted to the paper in the hopes that publication would increase sales of the originals. Russell also sent several views east, to *Frank Leslie's Illustrated Weekly*, although whether on his own initiative or at the request of the railroad officials is again unknown. *Harper's Weekly* printed one of Savage's views (fig. 40) of the two engines meeting on the tracks as a lithograph print (fig. 53).[30] Russell's nearly identical "East meets West" photo was used as a centerpiece in *Leslie's*, and two of his other images were reproduced on the front page.[31] In later years, as

Russell's view became more widely published, and original Savage images of Promontory became scarce, credit for Russell's Promontory photograph was given to Savage, based on the widespread recognition of the *Harper's Weekly* lithograph.

A number of authors have commented on the absence of champagne or beer bottles being held by the men on the engines in the *Harper's Weekly* lithograph. The assumption has often been made that the bottles were tastefully "edited out" when the lithograph was made. Careful comparison of the existing images confirms that the lithograph was faithfully copied from the original of figure 40. The champagne bottles are missing in this view, apparently blurred beyond recognition by movement of the men perched

FIGURE 54.
Engineer's camp at Weber Canyon with A. J. Russell leaning on a stereo camera, with his wagon to the right. From a stereoview by C. R. Savage. Collection of Barry Swackhamer.

on the engines during the long exposure.

Although newspaper publication of the Promontory pictures increased the reputation of the cameramen, it brought little financial reward, as newspapers of the day paid poorly, and often neglected to give adequate credit for photos. The sale of stereo cards and views to individuals provided the main source of income for most landscape photographers. Immediately after the Promontory celebration, Charles returned home to his studio to sell copies of the photographs. The images of this event sold very well locally, and he described in his journal (May 12, 1869) being "very busy in getting out pictures." He further stated that "my promontory views look first rate, and sales for views have amounted to $125 in 3 days."[32] There was a large demand for his images outside Utah as well, and he sent copies to a number of distributors for sale. This extra income went far toward helping him to pay off a number of debts, including a partial payment to E. and H. T. Anthony. His journal shows that within a few days of the completion of the railroad he was visited by a representative from Anthony's, to whom he paid $100, and gave a quantity of photographs that could be easily sold in the East to raise more cash.[33]

One month after the laying of the last rail, Charles took another trip to Echo, where he again joined Russell and spent several days photographing points of interest with him. Figure 54 is a photograph taken by Savage during this trip and is entitled "Engineer's Camp, Webers Canyon." It shows Russell's wagon on the right. The man leaning on the stereo camera and tripod is probably Russell himself. The many Savage and Russell images from the Utah area, taken from nearly identical positions and at almost the

FIGURE 55.
Old Stage Station, Echo, Utah, c. 1869. Charles Savage leaning against horse in foreground, A. J. Russell's photo wagon to the left. Stereoview in the collection of Union Pacific Railroad Museum.

same time, again suggests that the relationship between the two men was more than just passing acquaintance. In addition to photographing together, they also exchanged negatives and photo equipment.[34]

Russell's photographic assistant during 1869, "Professor" Stephen J. Sedgwick, was a travelling lecturer who went west in 1869 to obtain further material for his lecture series. Sedgwick also developed a friendship with Savage that summer, and continued to correspond with him until Savage's death.[35] Charles also visited Sedgwick, his "old acquaintance of early railroad days," on at least one occasion while on a trip to New York.[36]

After Russell's return to the East, his railroad negatives were acquired by O. C. Smith, Union Pacific paymaster and another of Savage's railroad friends.[37] The negatives later wound up in Sedgwick's hands. Both men sold prints under their own labels, without giving Russell credit. Sedgwick, who used lantern slides made from

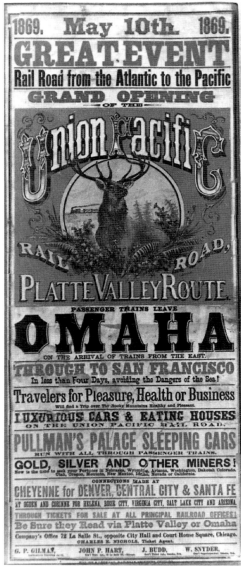

Russell's negatives in his lectures, credited the photos to "The Photographic Corps of the UPRR, of Which Prof. Sedgwick Was a Member."[38] There is, however, no evidence that such a corps ever existed, or that Sedgwick took a single photograph during the summer of 1869.[39]

In 1940 the glass-plate negatives, still in Russell's original wooden boxes, were given to the American Geographical Society,[40] and were later acquired by the Oakland Museum in California, where they now reside. In recent years, they have been recognized as Russell's by the handwritten titles scratched into the emulsion, and credit for the often reproduced "East meets West" photograph has been returned to the rightful photographer.

By the fall of 1869, eastern stereoscopic distributors were busily selling extensive collections of railroad pictures by a number of photographers. Frontier camera artists were drawn to other, less photographed sites, such as Yellowstone and Yosemite. Hart prospered for a while selling Promontory views, but was soon replaced as the official Central Pacific Railroad photographer by C. E. Watkins, who achieved fame by photo-documenting the Yosemite Valley. For many years Watkins published Hart's negatives under his own label, but they were eventually destroyed in the San Francisco earthquake of 1906.[41] Hart continued in photography for a time, but eventually returned to painting as a livelihood. Like many frontier photographers, he appears to have spent his later years in poverty, and when he died in 1908, his role in the Promontory celebrations had been all but forgotten.

Russell remained in the West during the summer and fall of 1869. He traveled on the railroad as far west as Sacramento in a limited photographic invasion of the Central Pacific territory, before returning to Echo, Utah. After the first snow, he worked his way back along the Union Pacific line, photographing the improvements made on the railroad. He eventually returned east to a permanent position with *Frank Leslie's Illustrated Weekly*, and died in New York in 1902.

These three men, who came together at the joining of the rails, struggled with the cumbersome technology of the time to photograph one of the most famous episodes in the history of the West. These images immortalized the coming of civilization to the western frontier—the end of an era. But even as the railroad whistles tolled the death of the Old West, Savage was preparing for new photographic excursions into the vanishing frontier.

NOTES

1. Letter in Fowler Family Papers; Brey, 41.
2. Although Captain Andrew Russell may have been working on salary from the Union Pacific, and later called himself "photo. to the UPPR," no official letters or payroll records exist to confirm his employment. Other photographers, such as J. B. Silvis and Charles Savage, used company private cars on photographic excursions, and many photographers were given free railroad passes in the hope of obtaining free publicity for the railroad.
3. Brey, 41.
4. Brey, 157.
5. Muster rolls of Company F, 141st Regiment, New York Infantry, War Department Records. No record exists of promotion beyond captain while in the service; however, Savage consistently referred to Russell as "Major" (Savage Journals, May 7, May 18, June 1, and June 5, 1869).
6. Russell, "Great Salt Lake City, Streetview," stereoview No. 24, copy in the UPRR Museum, Omaha, Nebraska.
7. Examples include Savage's "Near Tunnel No. 3, Weber" (compare with Russell No. 133 "On the Mountains of the Weber"); Savage's stereo "East Tunnel, Weber Valley" (compare Russell Stereo No. 73, "Tunnel No. 3, Weber Canyon" and Russell Oakland Museum, O.M. negative 121); and Savage's stereo "Grader's Camp" (compare Russell O.M. negative S-286a). Comparisons courtesy of Susan Williams, Oakland, California, a biographer of Russell who was the first to suggest the friendship

between Russell and Savage, which has been borne out by the existing journal and photographic records.

8. Russell, "Old Stage Station at Echo City," negative #S-357, Oakland Museum, California.

9. Examples include Savage's stereograph, "Conglomerate Rocks, Mouth of Echo," copy in the author's possession (compare to Russell stereo "No. 120—Stage Station, Hanging Rock, Echo Canyon," figure 54.

10. Original glass plate negatives in the collection of the Oakland Museum, California.

11. Willumsen, 63.

12. Willumsen, 68.

13. E. B. Crocker to Collis P. Huntington, August 2, 1867, Collis P. Huntington Papers.

14. George Reynolds to George F. Gibbs, June 4, 1868, in the *Millennial Star*, xxx (1868), 443.

15. Letter in Fowler Family Papers.

16. Savage Journals, April 20, 1869.

17. Savage Journals, May 4, 1869.

18. Jackson, 175.

19. Savage Journals, May 7, 1869.

20. Original stereograph in the collection of Barry Swackhamer, San Jose, California.

21. Best (p. 178) notes that the engine in the photo, No. 66, was built in August 1868, thus placing the photograph after this date. Savage's journal for 1868 is missing, but other existing images demonstrate that he was taking pictures of the UPRR construction in the fall of 1868.

22. Savage Journals, May 9, 1868.

23. Sabin, 218.

24. Bissell.

25. Sabin, 226.

26. Original stereo, "Meeting of Locomotives at Promontory," in the collection of Barry Swackhamer. Carte-de-visite prints from the same negative can be found in the Harold B. Lee Library at Brigham Young University and the Utah State Historical Society Archives in Salt Lake City. Figure 51 from the collection of Carl Mautz is also present as a stereoview in the Utah State Historical Society Collection.

27. Savage Journals, May 10, 1868.

28. For a description of most of the photographs taken by Savage at Promontory, with comparisons to similar images by Russell and Hart, see Richards. In addition to the eight Savage Promontory images shown in this chapter, the journals describe a picture of "Engine 119" and one or two other images taken on May 7, 1869.

29. Savage Journals, May 12, 1869.

30. *Harper's Weekly*, June 5, 1869.

31. *Leslie's Illustrated Weekly*, June 5, 1869.

32. Savage Journals, May 18, 1869.

33. Savage Journals, May 17, May 18, 1869.

34. Savage Journals, May 18, June 5, 1869.

35. Steven J. Sedgwick, Elmhurst, Queens, to C. R. Savage, April 12, 1907, Savage Scrapbook.

36. Savage Journals, October 12, 1889.

37. Savage Journals, June 1, 1869, February 14, 1884.

38. Sedgwick, "Catalogue of Stereoscopic views of Scenery." The title page of this sale catalog of photographs reads: "Catalogue of Stereoscopic views of Scenery in all parts of the Rocky Mountains, between Omaha and Sacramento, taken by the Photographic Corps of U.P.R.R., of which Prof. Sedgwick was a Member, for Union Pacific Railroad, at a cost of over $10,000."

39. Personal communication, Don Snoddy, UPRR Museum, Omaha, Nebraska, to author, regarding UPRR payroll and other records.

40. Pattison, 25.

41. Willumsen, 71.

CHAPTER 6

Frontier Photographer

NOT all of Savage's activities centered around railroads and photography. He was also interested in gardening, and his journal for the spring of 1869 is full of entries on the progress of the family garden. For Charles, as for most of the early Utah dwellers, the home garden was a necessity rather than a hobby, providing fresh produce for the family in season. Many families sold their extra produce, which afforded them a few "store-bought" luxuries. Charles attacked the enterprise with his usual scientific zeal. In addition to buying cuttings and seeds from nurseries across the country,[1] he kept careful records in his journal of the effects of various methods of planting and different weather conditions on his garden. This scientific approach was doubtless a legacy from his father, the English gardener and flower-breeder. The Savage garden included white and red grapes on running trellises in the back yard, and a small orchard contained peach, apricot, pear, apple, plum, and cherry trees. Bushes of raspberries, gooseberries, and black and English currants provided fruit to be bottled for the winter months. The kitchen garden provided corn, potatoes, peas, and lettuce, a great portion of which found its way into the homes of elderly neighbors.

With the completion of the railroad, Charles was busy in the gallery, printing the new Promontory views and other scenic views of the West. The easy access to Utah and the novelty of the new railroad brought large numbers of visitors to the city, many of whom stopped at Savage and Ottinger's to obtain souvenirs of their trip to the Mormon capital. In addition to landscape views, city scenes, and portraits of prominent Utah citizens, the enterprising cameraman sold vials of salt water and sand from the Great Salt Lake.

Only two months after the driving of the golden spike, a stranger walked into the Savage studio and asked to buy some cardboard on which to mount photographs. This visiting photographer was William Henry Jackson, who at that time was working his way through the West as an itinerant photographer in order to obtain a stock of negatives to boost his business. With an assistant named Hull, Jackson spent several months photographing scenes along the newly completed railway before returning home to his studio in Omaha. He reported that he obtained the cardboard he needed at "a stiff price,"[2] and spent a few minutes talking with Savage before continuing on his journey. Although at that time a virtual unknown, Jackson later became perhaps the most famous of all western landscape photographers of the nineteenth century, mainly for his work in photo-documenting the Yellowstone area as part of Hayden's geologic survey of 1871. Jackson served as staff photographer for the Hayden surveys from 1870-1879, and the photographs produced during these trips were instrumental in convincing Congress to establish Yellowstone as the country's first national park.

In the latter half of the nineteenth century, the federal government funded a number of surveys, all intended to explore the new territory west of the Missouri River. These

FIGURE 57. (OPPOSITE)
Members of Hayden's U.S.G.S. Survey, Snake River Department. Albumen print, by William Henry Jackson, 1872. Collection of Alison Taggart.

expeditions were generally geologic surveys, with an emphasis on discovering mineral reserves for development and providing maps of unexplored areas. The leaders of these expeditions were usually men of broad interests, however, such as Ferdinand V. Hayden, Clarence King, and John Wesley Powell. These men assembled teams of explorers whose interests included geology, zoology, botany, general science, and the ethnology of the American Indian. The surveys, therefore, accumulated much valuable information about the West prior to its civilization.

Photography was rarely a part of the early expeditions, due to the limitations of the daguerreotype process, although a few men successfully photographed on surveys with this method. By the end of the 1860s, the advantages of the wet-plate process were evident, and the presence of a cameraman was considered almost mandatory. Expedition leaders quickly learned the value of photographs to complement their reports to their supervising agencies. The surveys were funded by the government on an annual basis, and pictures of the wild country covered by the expeditions were very helpful in gaining funding for future expeditions.

In 1869, the "Fortieth Parallel Survey," headed by Clarence King, passed through Utah. This three-year expedition was to cover the region between Virginia City, Nevada, and Denver, Colorado, reporting on "the minerals, flora, and the fauna of the country, and its agricultural capacity."[3] This was the first federal exploring party in the West since the Civil War, and King chose T. H. O'Sullivan, a veteran of Civil War photography, as the main photographer. O'Sullivan was a confirmed explorer and frontier photographer, and spent time behind a camera in such inhospitable regions as Panama and the American desert southwest.

Savage first met O'Sullivan in May of 1869, while the geologic survey was camped on the foothills above Salt Lake City. In early June, he headed for Big Cottonwood Canyon east of Salt Lake in company with O'Sullivan and other members of the survey. He spent a week with O'Sullivan taking pictures, and some of the images taken by Charles are nearly identical to those taken by his companion. Eventually the expedition headed into the Uinta Range, and Savage returned to Salt Lake City.

Other geologic expeditions and surveys crossed and re-crossed the western United States in that era. To the south, Major John Wesley Powell began his epic journeys down the Colorado River and into the Grand Canyon. Powell's photographer for his second expedition was E. O. Beaman. In the fall of 1871, Powell walked into Savage's studio in Salt Lake, and asked James Fennemore, one of Savage's employees, to print 250 pictures taken by Beaman during his recent river trip from Green River, Wyoming, to what is now Green River, Utah. Powell needed these pictures to help convince Washington congressmen to fund further exploration. He was so pleased with the printing that he asked Fennemore to join the expedition the following year as photographer-in-chief. During this next expedition, a young member of the group by the name of John K. Hillers expressed an interest in learning photography. Fennemore gladly taught him, and Hillers, with a natural ability in this area, soon equaled his teacher. As the team prepared to begin a new river voyage down the Grand Canyon in the summer of 1872, Fennemore was taken ill, and was unable to continue. Hillers was promoted to photographer-in-chief for the trip,[4] and became the official photographer of the Powell expeditions, a position which he held from 1872 to 1878.

As the year 1870 began, Charles was called upon to perform more railroad photography. The Utah Central Railroad was completed on January 10 of that year, and Savage was there to record the moment on glass. He already had negatives of the groundbreaking ceremonies taken the previous year by Andrew Russell,[5] but he recognized the local sales potential of photographs of this exclusively Mormon project. The Utah Central was a spur joining the Union Pacific line, and connected Salt Lake City to Ogden by rail. This short road had been built using steel and rolling stock obtained from the Union Pacific in trade. The original Union Pacific contracts to grade and tunnel east of Promontory had never been completely paid; the high-rolling financial schemes of Durant and other Union Pacific financiers had left the company unable or unwilling to pay cash for the debt. Despite legal battles, only a fraction of the money due the Mormon subcontractors was ever paid, much of this in materials and rolling stock used for the Utah Central Railroad. With the completion of this road, many Salt Lakers felt truly connected with the rest of the nation for the first time. Charles recorded the final ceremonies of the Utah Central completion in his journal:

January 10, 1870. Grand finale to track laying. President B. Young drove the last spike. Many visitors came from different points. Everything passed off very lively and pleasant. Took 2 photos of the ceremony. Speeches were delivered by G. Q. Cannon, Morris of UPRR and others. Thirty-six guns were fired, one for each mile of the road. In the evening we attended a great ball in the Theater, there was present most of the citizens of this City and Camp Douglas. Our children saw the trains and locomotives for the first time.

Soon after, Charles received a pleasant surprise—he was invited to join Brigham Young and his party on his annual visit to the southern colonies of Utah. This was an opportunity he had long desired, and it may well have been occasioned by his studio photography of the Prophet and his growing local reputation as a public speaker. For many years, Brigham Young had made a spring tour of the outlying Mormon communities in the Utah Territory. This provided an important link to the frontier towns, and was eagerly awaited by settlers in these colonies.

On February 25, Savage headed south with the rest of Brigham Young's party on a six-week road trip to Utah's "Dixie," which carried the group as far afield as the junction of the Colorado River and the Rio Virgin, some 450 miles south of Salt Lake City. At each settlement the party stayed overnight, renewed old acquaintances, and held meetings. Charles was asked to give short talks in some of these meetings. At most towns, settlers lined the roadside to wave and cheer the arrival of their prophet.

Charles later wrote a three-part account of this experience for the L.D.S. church magazine *Improvement Era*. This article, "A Trip South with President Young in 1870," gives an excellent character portrayal of Brigham Young, in addition to an interesting description of pioneer life in rural Utah. President Young was called upon in each town to deliver a sermon, which usually focused on the exigencies of daily life as a

FIGURE 59.
Beaver, Utah. Cabinet card, c. 1870, by James Fennemore. Collection of L.D.S. Church Archives.

FIGURE 60.
Temples of the Rio Virgin. View from the Zion Canyon trip, from a stereoview by C. R. Savage, 1870. Collection of Bradley Richards.

FIGURE 61.
Cottonwood Canyon, wagon camp scene. From a stereoview by C. R. Savage, c. 1870. Probably part of the geologic survey headed into the Wasatch Mountains. Collection of the L.D.S. Church Archives.

Christian on the frontier farms rather than on deep doctrinal subjects. On one occasion he was asked to settle a dispute between several local Indians, an anecdote Charles relates in his article. The Indians chose "Bigam," as they called him, to act as mediator, since "they said he never talked 'forked,' always 'straight.'"

Savage's role was not only that of a spectator. He took his "photographic apparatus" on the trip, and used it. On one occasion he made a picture of the party of Church officials, with Brigham Young seated in the center. Later in the trip, he split off from the main group to photograph a small valley off the Virgin River known as Little Zion Valley (now Zion National Park). "It was given out as a remarkable fact," Charles wrote, "that thousands could find a hiding place up there, so my ambition was aroused to see it."

Some enthusiasts had reported the place to President Young as a veritable Zion. "Call it Little Zion," said he, and that is the name it still bears.

I found it to be a remarkable valley with high, vertical cliffs, towering upward from two to three thousand feet, and so completely locked that there was no outlet other than the way of entrance. From a picturesque point of view, it was grand, sublime, and majestic, but as a place of residence, lonely and unattractive, reminding one of living in a stone box; the landscape, a skyscrape; a good place to visit, and a nice place to leave. The whole region of the headwaters of the Rio Virgin is very beautiful for the artist, and the river banks afford good places for settlers.

During the course of this trip through Zion Canyon, Savage records having taken sixteen views at various sites in the canyon. These photographs were the first pictures ever made of Zion Park, now the most popular and photographed of Utah's national parks. These images preceded by two years those taken by the Powell expedition.[6] Charles took another photographic trip to Zion Canyon in 1875, but at that time complained that, although the canyon was beautiful, it "disappoints an artist, being too lofty and no distance to be set from the object to be got."[7]

By a strange twist of fate, one of Savage's grandsons was intimately involved with Zion's Park seventy years later. This grandson, Harrison Brothers, was the military leader in charge of the construction of the Civilian Conservation Corps camps in the Zion Canyon area. These camps housed the teams that built the roads and tunnels through Zion Park.[8]

When the party reached Beaver City, sad news awaited Savage. His youngest son, Enos Hoge Savage, only five months old, had taken ill. Charles hurried home by stage and found his worst fears realized. Within a few days of his arrival home, the child passed away. Friends of the family rallied around to comfort the grieving parents, and Charles asked George Ottinger to paint a picture of the boy to comfort Annie. She cried nearly every night until the birth of their next child, Luacine.[9] Charles found consolation in his work—within a month, he was off on another trip to California, followed soon after by a repeat trip to the Uintas.

In November of 1870, Charles became embroiled in a bizarre chapter of the history of Utah, an episode later known as the "Wooden Gun Rebellion." This strange event revolved around his membership in the State Militia, and his leadership of the militia's musical band.

In the aftermath of the Utah War, and with the rise of anti-polygamy sentiment, a number of bills were introduced into Congress that aimed at reducing the political power held by the Mormon Church in Utah. Brigham Young was removed as the governor of Utah Territory, and replaced with federally appointed officials, one of whom was Governor Shaffer. Several bills introduced into Congress contained the provision to place the Territorial Militia under the direct and complete control of the governor, rather than the legislature, as in other states and territories. Had such a bill passed, it would have presented a serious constitutional question, and the U.S. Supreme Court would have been called on to decide whether such unilateral power could be placed in the hands of the governor of a Territory. None of the bills passed both houses. In spite of this, Governor Shaffer issued a proclamation disbanding the militia, relieving its officers of their command, and declaring that any gathering of any branch of the militia would be construed as an overt act of treason and rebellion against the United States Government. Soon after issuing this proclamation, Governor Shaffer died and was replaced by Vernon H. Vaughn, former Secretary of the Territory of Utah. George A. Black assumed the position of Secretary. Although Governor Shaffer was dead, his proclamation was still in force.

In the meantime, the 3rd Regimental Band had received some new musical instruments from the East, and like any band with new instruments, wanted to try them out. The band was a new one, comprised mostly of young men and boys who had only recently been organized and taught to play. Charles served as their band leader. Some controversy exists as to whether what followed was a deliberate test of an uncon-

stitutional and illegal policy, or simply an oversight. According to the popular version, the band met at the Twentieth Ward Schoolhouse for an impromptu concert, and a good portion of the regiment turned out to march to the music. It is said that they "had an very pleasant time together, and were all exceedingly pleased with the music of the band and also with their own evolutions."[10] Many neighbors came out to hear the music and see the men in uniform. Most of the young men in the regiment did not have real guns to carry in the drill, and used wooden guns or sticks in place of the genuine article, thereby lending a name to the event.

When news of the drill reached the governor's office, Secretary Black, an avid anti-Mormon, hurried to the scene with two deputy marshals. With the aid of a witness named Richard Keyes, he took down the names of the principal officers of the regiment. Immediately after the dismissal of the regiment, a warrant was issued for the arrest of eight regimental officers, including Savage, George Ottinger, and James Fennemore, Savage's assistant.[11] The charges were "treason, insurrection, and inciting to insurrection," based solely on their non-compliance with the late Governor Shaffer's proclamation. The men were arraigned before Associate Justice Cyrus M. Hawley, who heard lengthy testimony from a number of witnesses. After deliberation, Judge Hawley bound the officers over to the next meeting of the Grand Jury, fixing bail at $5000 or $2000, depending on rank.[12] While waiting for their bail, the militia officers were kept under house arrest at Fort Douglas in the officer's quarters, where they were allowed to receive visitors. The incident had made the men local heroes, and there was a steady stream of visitors bearing gifts. Supportive local merchants provided

FIGURE 62.
Utah Militia band, stereoview by C. R. Savage, c. 1875. Collection of L.D.S. Church Archives.

FIGURE 63.
Utah Militia officers, stereoview by C. R. Savage, c. 1875. Collection of L.D.S. Church Archives.

the prisoners with food and delicacies. While confined at Fort Douglas, Charles and his fellow officers, clearly in high spirits, composed a song to satirize the episode, sung to the tune of "Sweet Betsy from Pike":

THE MILITIA-MAN'S LAMENT

My friends, a sad story I'm going to tell
Of a doleful misfortune that to me befell.
You see, a good soldier I resolved for to be
But wicked old Hawley, he grabbed hold of me.

Chorus: Singing tooral-li ooral-li etc. With long wooden guns and a feather or two
And an ancient brass coat with buttons so blue
I armed myself, as the law books do say
And to the parade ground I hastened away.
Chorus

From one to ten hundred together we got.
The general started out I don't know what
When Secretary Black in a buggy drew near
And took down my name, then I felt very queer.
Chorus

Now a trap had been set, for such is the tale
But 'twas sprung by a mouse instead of a whale.
Marshal Patrick nabbed me, thinks I: that looks squally
And I'm blest if he didn't haul me up before old Judge Hawley.
Chorus

Away to Camp Douglas they carried me straight
There to be confined as a prisoner of state
And made me give bonds to keep true and firm
Till the grand jury sits on its next March term.

The words to this song were later written down by Savage at the request of "Brother Chambers." The manuscript has a postscript stating: "It is not very neatly copied but I think you will be able to decipher it and correct any omissions I may have been guilty of—the verses are all there and your memory will tide you over some of the obscure paragraphs." [13]

B. H. Roberts, the noted L.D.S. historian, styled the Wooden Gun Rebellion as a "comic opera" in Utah's history.[14] In their zeal to suppress the political power of the L.D.S. Church, the federal appointees had jailed a neighborhood marching band and charged its members with treason and insurrection. Perhaps understanding the appearance that this action would have under closer examination by their superiors, the governor and his staff were content to let the issue die quietly. When the Grand Jury met, it refused to indict the prisoners on any charge.

Charles never wrote publicly regarding his role in the Wooden Gun Rebellion, and even his journal is silent on the subject. Whether he called his young band out under orders to test the governor's proclamation, or simply as a social activity will probably never be known. But, as leader of the band, his decision to gather the group that day placed him in a pivotal role in this unusual chapter of Utah's history.

By the mid 1870s, the fame and success of the Savage studio was at its peak. Business was booming in Salt Lake City, and the tourists arriving on the railroad were frequent visitors to Savage's Pioneer Art Gallery. Charles tore down his five-room adobe house and built a larger wood frame structure on the same site to house his growing family. (The house still stands today at 80 D Street in Salt Lake City.) "I find myself about $700 in debt on building my

FIGURE 64.
Savage's second home on 80 D street. Photograph by C. R. Savage, c. 1880-90. From Savage Book of Remembrance.

house, which is very gratifying," he wrote. "I am steadily reducing my debt at the bank and in the States. Business growing better steadily. . . . Have in my employ 8 individuals, paying now $100 per week for wages." The new house included a large room to the rear that served as "Charlie's Gallery." There he exhibited the many paintings he had acquired from local artists—some as gifts, others in trade for art supplies, food, and shelter.

Many artists of early Utah, as elsewhere, found it difficult to earn a living at their trade. Charles saw the cultural necessity of promoting art among the Saints, and realized that a community with a tradition of art appreciation would form a better clientele for his own business. But most importantly, his compassion prompted him to help those in need. He often traded art supplies, food, or even cash for paintings, many of which he knew he could never sell, and for years he let homeless artists sleep in the upper rooms of his studio without charge. One such painter, weakened by hunger and exposure before seeking help, died in the loft of Savage's gallery.[15]

With business on the increase, the Old Pioneer Art Gallery became too cramped. In 1875 Charles replaced it with a new structure named the "Art Bazar." On October 6 the new gallery

FIGURE 65.
Salt Lake City Temple grounds with Savage's new studio shown in the foreground to the left. Albumen print by C. R. Savage, c. 1881. Collection of L.D.S. Church Archives.

was featured in an article in the *Deseret News*, with an interesting and detailed description of the building:

> The present building, now nearly completed, is one that the city will be proud of, as it clearly shows that Utah is making a steady growth in art development, greatly in advance of the territories around her. . . .
>
> The Art Bazar above referred to is erected on the site of the Old Pioneer. It is 100 feet deep by 28 feet wide. The first story is 14 feet in the clear, and the second story 12 feet, with large glass front, and fine attractive windows on the second story. The showroom, on the first floor, is 60 feet long, with a spacious staircase leading to the second story. The balance of the first story is divided into a picture frame room, 13 x 39 feet, office, photograph mounting and burnishing room; next a photograph washing room, where the mysteries of toning and fixing the prints are attended to.
>
> On ascending the stairway to the second story, you are received in a fine reception room connected with a ladies dressing room, artist's room, and fine operating room 26 x 39 feet, with skylight and sidelight, 16 x 20 feet, connected with a roomy dark room or chemical room, dark room being a misnomer, as the sensitive negative can be subjected to a flood of light, provided it is non-actinic, as the scientists say. The balance of the floor is used for printing photographs, a very interesting and curious operation.
>
> It will be seen that a person can get his portrait taken, and have the frame made on the spot by skilled artizans, and the new Bazar admits of doing everything first class,

none but competent persons to be employed. Another feature is the mounting, varnishing, and framing of chromos, in the same building. The chromos are received in sheet form and turned into the show room fit for any parlor in the land. In the second story is stored a vast collection of negative views, the result of ten years' hard travelling of Mr. Savage, reaching all over the West, Colorado, Wyoming, Idaho, Montana, Arizona, Utah, Nevada, and California being well represented. . . .

> On the walls of the show room are paintings from the easels of G. M. Ottinger, F. Lambourne, and others of our home artists.

A photograph of the Salt Lake Temple grounds (fig. 65) shows the new Art Bazar in the left foreground. The skylight windows faced north, as was the custom in those days, in order to catch the diffused northern light for the photographic studio. Next to the Art Bazar, also to the north, is the old Council House.

In the late 1870s Charles spent more and more time traveling by rail in search of photographic opportunities. He photographed along the Denver and Rio Grande Western, Union Pacific, Central Pacific, Utah Central, and other western railroads. All of the railroads gave him free passes, which opened up the entire nation to him. He made frequent trips to the East and West coasts. On several occasions in later years he was supplied with a private car for photographic use.[16] This was an unheard of luxury for a photographer, as private cars were generally reserved for railroad executives or the extremely wealthy. Savage wrote of one of these trips:

> No mode of traveling on a railway is more

agreeable than a private car. It is the traveling office of the railroad magnate, and his home wherever he goes. In howling storms and whenever the elements call for his presence, in times of accidents, washouts and other mishaps, it is a comfortable shelter. When everything is lovely and all smooth sailing it is the ne plus ultra of pleasant life on the rail.

Our private car contained a kitchen, dining room, comfortable bedrooms, and observation room; everything was served up as nicely as it could have been in a first-class hotel. I am not astonished that other millionaires besides myself enjoy them, noted aspirants for office, operatic stars, all affect private cars, and I really do not blame them.[17]

The reason for this unprecedented liberality was very simple. As one of the best known western scenic photographers in the country, his photographs along the train routes were widely distributed, and were good publicity. His "Views of the Great West" were published as a stereo collection, and were often reproduced in travel brochures and pamphlets by the railroads. In addition, he usually wrote glowing reports of the service aboard the trains for the Salt Lake City newspapers, and never failed to send copies of pictures and other souvenirs to railroad officers. This thoughtfulness was extended to all the railroad men Charles met, from the president of the company down to the switchmen in rural stations. These many kindnesses not only earned him free train passes, but the respect of railroad men throughout the West.

On at least one occasion, Charles tried to help the railroads with suggestions for improvement. In 1875 in an interview with an official of one of the railroad companies, he suggested that electricity be used for train headlights and for lighting in passenger cars, rather than the dangerous gas lamps.[18] This advice was too far ahead of its time, however, and trains did not incorporate electric lights for nearly two more decades.

During one photographic trip on the Denver and Rio Grande Western Railroad, Charles named the Royal Gorge in central Colorado. Apparently when Savage saw the canyon for the first time, he exclaimed "This is a royal gorge!" The railroad company needed a name for the Gorge when the photographs were published in their travel brochures, and used the title suggested by his remark, and the canyon has been known as Royal Gorge ever since.

Savage often traveled with local artists, such as Fred Lambourne, John Hafen, and George Ottinger, who sketched and painted while Charles photographed. He also convinced the railroad companies to provide free passes for his artist friends.[19] In addition to these railroad trips, Savage often made pack trips into the more remote areas of the West with his artistic companions. In later years, Charles often traveled with one of his sons, especially on business trips to California or the East.

On one trip to San Francisco, Charles stopped to visit an old friend, Fannie Stenhouse. She and her husband, T. B. H. Stenhouse, had moved to California after their excommunication from the L.D.S. Church, and were living off the royalties of anti-Mormon books. Although not unfriendly to Charles, she spoke bitterly against the church.

She commenced by inquiring after my family, and if I had another wife, &c., &c. When I told her the facts, she gave me a short venomous harangue against everything

FIGURE 66.
Logo of the stereoview series, "Views of the Great West," C. R. Savage, c. 1878. Collection of Harrison Brothers.

FIGURE 67.
L.D.S. religious services on the beach near the Cliff House, San Francisco, May 23, 1897. Albumen photograph, taken by John Todd at Savage's request. Collection of L.D.S. Church Archives.

Mormon, and Polygamy in particular. She stated that she had become infidel to all religions. She talked like any woman would that was opposed to the Mormon faith, said that her husband had given up to drink since he left the Church. And that she was supporting the family, and that her prospects were good now . . . that she would like to live in Utah. That she thought a good deal of many persons there, spoke of my wife in the most endearing manner, how much she loved her, &c., &c. . . . After a little desultory talk of a light character, a Mr. Hyde, brother of Julian Hyde came into the room to keep an appointment. I withdrew, with the reflection that whatever success she had had in pulling down the Mormon faith, it had not been a source of comfort to her, that when people have any friendship toward me it will manifest itself in respecting what I hold sacred. I think I shall not trouble her again—such friendship is not what I seek.[20]

A year later, however, Charles visited her again, and found her "more agreeable, and less vinegar in her talk than a year ago."[21] She expressed a desire to be near her old friends in Salt Lake City, but neither she nor her husband ever rejoined the Church or returned to Utah.

In 1876, Charles traveled to Chicago for the Centennial World's Fair, where he spent a month viewing exhibits that ranged from new

FIGURE 68.
Artist Fred Lambourne (holding palette) on an excursion with Savage in a Denver-Rio Grande Western private railway car. Annie Savage is seated next to Lambourne. Albumen print by C. R. Savage, c. 1893. Collection of L.D.S. Church Archives.

THE SAVAGE VIEW

technology to dinosaur bones. His journal lists books to buy, ideas for future talks, and descriptions of exhibits. He began entering his own photographs in world fairs, and always entered them in Utah's annual Territorial Fair. He received medals nearly every year in the local fairs in various categories of photography, and occasionally garnered a national medal as well.

Savage's gallery brought him into contact with thousands of tourists who stopped there to buy souvenirs, but very few ever wrote of the visit. One of these few was Mrs. Frank Leslie, the wife of the prominent New York newspaper editor, who traveled from New York to San Francisco. She wrote an account of her trip, entitled *California, a Pleasure Trip from Gotham to the Golden Gate,* which was illustrated with a number of engravings, some of which may have been based on photos obtained from the Art Bazar. While in the "City of the Saints," Mrs. Leslie visited with Savage, and wrote of her impressions of their conversation:

Reaching the principal photographer, who was an old acquaintance of our Chief's, we paid him a visit, and found a good assortment of views of the city and its surroundings, and a very civil and gentlemanlike proprietor, who seemed quite amiably willing to impart the information we were thirsting to obtain. He freely admitted himself to be a Mormon, somewhat defiantly stating that he had nailed his colors to the mast. A picture of the Beehive, Brigham Young's principal residence, easily led to a discussion of Mormon houses and Mormon domesticity. But our new friend considered it very unlikely that we, even the women of the party, would be able to interview any of the upper class of Mormon wives. "The ladies here don't like being made subjects of curiosity," said he. "Their homes are just as sacred to them as yours in the East are to you, and they are very sensitive about being questioned." Then he cited, evidently as a timely warning, the case of a titled English lady recently passing through Utah, and remarkable, as our photographer seemed to think, in possessing more than the usual amount of cheek—"as much cheek as a government mule"—some artistic effect of which feature probably attracted his professional eye. This lady, as it seemed, possessed the troublesome characteristic of "wanting to know, you know," and attempted to gratify it in an artless manner by calling upon several of the Mormon ladies, and putting them to their catechism with the vigorous candor of a parish visitor. The consequence was that Miladi got terribly snubbed, and what was perhaps worse, learned nothing, and went away the next day to make up her notes of travel as best she could. Having furnished this little narrative, our friend paused significantly, with a *Haec fabula docet* air, and then indulgently added: "But I'll give you an introduction to the leading Mormon editor of the city, and you can see what he will do for you." Then he showed us some portraits of the various Mesdames Young, first of the recreant Ann Eliza, who "bolted," as he phrased it, upon the very day the President was about to present her with the title-deeds of the house she lived in. "And here's the house," continued he, producing a picture of a neat little villa; "that's the hovel she talks about in the East." When President Young was informed that she was gone, or at least

FIGURE 69.
Amelia Palace, the home of one of Brigham Young's wives in Salt Lake City. Albumen print by C. R. Savage, c. 1890. Collection of Utah State Historical Society.

FIGURE 70.
Eagle Gate and Bee Hive House by C. R. Savage,
c. 1875. Albumen print. Collection of Bradley Richards.

had removed with all her effects to the Walker House—the Gentile hotel, you know—he just opened his desk, took out the "title-deeds," and, tearing them across, said quietly: "So much saved!"

The next picture represented a lady of about thirty, well dressed, a little stout, with a strong, sensible, pleasing face, and something of a stylish air. This was Mrs. Amelia, said to be Mr. Young's favorite wife, but this assumption our photographer scouted indignantly. "That was only Eastern talk; there was a lot of nonsense talked in the East about the Mormons, and Ann Eliza had set a whole

raft of stories afloat, but all about it was that Mrs. Amelia was a born nurse, and had taken care of Mr. Young through some bad times, and so he always took her traveling with him and liked to have her near him at home." To a delicate suggestion about selling Amelia's picture, the artist shook his head; no, he couldn't sell that or the picture of any private lady. He had been offered a hundred dollars for it, but it was not for sale. We appreciated the fine feeling of this little speech, and mentally wondered how long our friend's position in Salt Lake City would be tenable if he offended Mrs. Amelia, and whether a hundred dollars would make up his loss in that case. On the whole, we concluded that he was a wise as well as an amusing and instructive photographer, and so took our leave.

Clearly the subject uppermost on the minds of many tourists to Salt Lake City in the '70s was that of polygamy. The Beehive House (Brigham Young's residence) was a subject of morbid curiosity among the eastern visitors, and many bought photographs of the building from Savage to take home. Polygamy was an institution that incited great derision and persecution of the Mormons. It was also an issue that would directly affect the life of C. R. Savage.

NOTES

1. Savage Journals, April 3, 1869.
2. Jackson, 181.
3. *New York Times*, May 8, 1867.
4. Frederick S. Dellenbaugh, in Kate B. Carter, vol. 18, 289.
5. Savage Journals, May 18, 1869.
6. Fowler, 185-186.
7. Savage Journals, May 15, 1875.
8. Personal communication, Harrison Brothers to the author, May 19, 1993.
9. Clark, *Life Sketch of Annie Adkins Savage.*
10. Tullidge, 495.
11. The other men arrested were Andrew Burt, Archibald Livingston, Charles Livingston, W. G. Phillips, and John C. Graham.
12. Roberts, 5:355.
13. Original in the Savage Scrapbook. The manuscript contains other verses to the song, which were eliminated for the sake of brevity.
14. Roberts, 5:355.
15. Benion.
16. Savage Journals, September 3, 1889, and June 8, 1893; *Deseret Evening News*, October 13, 1900.
17. Savage, "A Sportsman's Paradise."
18. Savage Journals, September 25, 1878.
19. San Pedro, Los Angeles and Salt Lake railroad to C. R. Savage, September 21, 1907, Brigham Young University Archives. The letter confirms a 1000-mile railroad passbook given to John Hafen, to be used within the state of Utah, and is one of several examples of such intervention by Savage on behalf of Utah artists. It also acknowledges the gift of some Indian pictures and an Indian pipe given to the president of the company by Savage.
20. Savage Journals, June 22, 1877.
21. Savage Journals, March 9, 1878.

CHAPTER 7

Family Life

THE L.D.S. doctrine of plural marriage became a personal matter for Charles and Annie in 1876, when Charles took a second wife, twenty four-year-old Mary Emma Fowler (fig. 71). Mary Fowler was born December 26, 1851, in Sheffield, Yorkshire, England, and came to America in 1863. On October 12, 1876, she was married to Charles Savage, a man twenty years her senior.

This must have been a great trial to both Charles and Annie. Theirs had been a wonderful marriage, and through journal entries and letters it is clear that the two adored each other. To have their tranquil lives interrupted by a plural marriage was difficult to accept. Two decades before, in a letter to his sweetheart prior to their marriage, Savage had written: "This much I think you believe of me—that I love this work and that I am ready to do anything for it."[1] Now he was being taken at his word. For a faithful Latter-day Saint like Charles or Annie, such an assignment was a call from the Lord, to be obeyed regardless of the personal sacrifice involved. And, like all the previous church assignments extended to the couple, it was accepted.

Mary Fowler, too, must have felt trepidation at entering into a twenty-year-old marriage as a third partner. Exactly what she felt or, indeed, what any of them experienced, can be only imagined, since no records exist to inform us of their daily lives in this arrangement. All we know is that Mary Fowler came to live at 80 D Street, and died in 1881, only five years later, of "a lingering illness" known at that time as "pelvic cellulitis."[2] No children were born of this union, probably because of the disease that cost Mary her life. Three years before she died, a third wife had been sealed to Savage, Ellen Fenn of Bedfordshire, England (fig. 72).[3]

Ellen Fenn was a cousin of Annie Adkins on her mother's side. At her marriage in 1878, she was a 35-year-old spinster.[4] Family tradition states that Annie Savage strongly encouraged this third marriage when it was suggested, since the intended bride, in addition to being a relative, was so unattractive that she was unlikely to find a husband elsewhere.[5] Family members have also suggested that, in Annie's mind at least, a homely wife might be more attractive in a plural marriage than a pretty one. Regardless of personal motives or feelings, this second plural marriage was accepted as was the first. Ellen Fenn lived in the Savage household for several years, and bore two children to Charles: Arley Fenn Savage and Emma Jane Savage. As national opposition toward the Mormon practice of plural marriage hardened into federal statute, Savage moved his third wife to a separate home in Provo, Utah, forty miles to the south. Here she lived with her two children, supported financially by Charles. Her children later returned to live in the Salt Lake City home while attending the University of Utah. Both halves of the family got along well with each other, and Annie's children always enjoyed visiting their "Aunt Ellen."

In the 1860s, an estimated ten percent of all Mormon families in Utah were polygamous.[6] Most of these were two-wife families,

FIGURE 71. (OPPOSITE)
Mary Emma Fowler, Savage's second wife, carte-de-visite, by C. R. Savage, c. 1877. Savage Book of Remembrance.

rather than the large harems commonly lampooned in eastern newspapers. The second wife of these families was usually a homeless immigrant, a spinster, or the wife of a deceased relative with a family to support. Assigning these women to husbands in plural marriages provided them with homes and support. It is, therefore, not surprising that the majority of plural marriages were solemnized in 1846 (the year of the Saints' expulsion from Illinois), and 1856 (the year of Utah's major drought and famine).[7] Contrary to the popular view of the time, these polygamous marriages were neither forced upon the parties involved nor sought after. Although at times difficult to accept, they were viewed as Church assignments, required by God and sanctioned by His holy Prophet.

In the East, however, the situation was viewed differently. The eastern press carried articles deprecating what was seen as a barbaric and unholy practice. Political cartoons depicted Mormon men pandering to a new, young wife, while older wives and children lived in squalor and despair. Sensational fictional accounts were written of young women stolen away from their families and forced into unwilling concubinage with lecherous old men. To counter these views, Mormons pointed out the liberal, progressive nature of life in Utah, and the freedoms enjoyed by women in the Territory. Women's suffrage began in Utah, they reasoned, and Utah was the first territory in the Union to allow women to vote. The Relief Society in Utah was one of the first organizations in the world founded and run solely by women.[8] Further, they argued, the women in polygamous marriages were all involved voluntarily, and enjoyed financial and social advantages that would be denied a woman in similar circumstances elsewhere in the United States. The absence in Mormon communities of the dual evils of prostitution and poverty was often invoked as a direct result of the Mormon's social structure.

These arguments did little, however, to stem the growing tide of opposition to Mormon polygamy. As early as the 1860s a series of restrictive laws were introduced before the legislature to limit plural marriage in Utah. The Anti-Bigamy Act of 1862 provided penalties for plural marriage, and disincorporated the L.D.S. Church. It further stated that any property held by the church in excess of $50,000 would be forfeit to the United States. The object of this bill was to "prevent the accumulation of wealth in the hands of theocratic institutions inconsistent with our form of government."[9]

Although the law was clearly unconstitutional, the church feigned compliance by placing most of its assets in the hands of private individuals known to be faithful to the L.D.S. Church. Participants in plural marriages also had only one civil marriage, the rest being "sealings," performed as church (not civil) ceremonies, making it difficult for federal marshals to prove marriage in cases of suspected bigamy. The Cullom Bill was introduced in 1869 to close these loopholes. It provided for all jurors in polygamy cases to be selected by the U.S. marshal and U.S. attorney, and for all such cases to be tried by federal judges. Plural wives were to be deprived of immunity as witnesses against husbands, and "cohabitation" (distinct from polygamy) was declared a misdemeanor. The Cullom Bill was narrowly defeated.

The Poland Act was passed in 1874. This act transferred all jurisdiction over criminal and civil cases in Utah to federal judges, and gave them considerable leeway in selecting jurors. This was

FIGURE 72.
Ellen Fenn, Savage's third wife. Albumen print by C. R. Savage, c. 1888. Savage Book of Remembrance.

THE SAVAGE VIEW

FIGURE 73.
Mormon men incarcerated under anti-polygamy laws, George Q. Cannon seated in doorway. Utah State Penitentiary in Sugar House, Utah. Albumen print by C. R. Savage, circa 1887. Collection of Utah State Historical Society.

upheld by the Supreme Court in 1879. In 1881, the Supreme Court pointed out several weaknesses in anti-polygamy legislation, which prompted the introduction of the Edmunds Act in 1882. This act imposed heavy penalties for polygamy, defined cohabitation as a misdemeanor subject to a $300 fine, six months imprisonment, or both, and declared all people found guilty of polygamy or cohabitation forfeit of their citizenship, unfit for jury service, and barred from public office. A five-man "Utah Commission" was appointed by the president to regulate elections and voter registration. As a matter of practical administration, the Utah Commission interpreted the Edmunds Act to mean that any person professing a belief in polygamy or cohabitation as a religious principle (i.e. any Mormon) was ineligible to vote or hold public office. The Utah Commission reported that in its first year of existence it excluded 12,000 Mormons from registration and voting.[10]

Savage never mentioned his own involvement with plural marriage in his journals, an understandable precaution, given the legal climate of the time. But when the Edmunds Act passed in 1883, he wrote bitterly:

> The Edmunds Bill has become law. I am no longer a citizen. My vote is taken from me and the right to hold office of trust politically is taken from me. I submit. But my satisfaction as a citizen of the U.S. is gone. I

look with pride upon the government of Old England more than ever. . . . Business as yet unaffected by the passing of the bill. But the future looks ominous.[11]

Business in Salt Lake City did slow dramatically after this bill was passed. With most of the leaders of the Church in hiding, and many of the male members of the city in prison, businesses faltered and most families in Utah were affected economically. For Charles, this drop in the local economy was somewhat offset by the rising numbers of tourists passing through the city, which kept the Art Bazar financially stable.

There was little question among the Mormons that the Edmunds Bill was unconstitutional, as it contradicted the First Amendment: "Congress shall make no law respecting the establishment of religion or interfering with the free exercise thereof." It was, therefore, challenged in the Supreme Court. On March 3, 1885, the Supreme Court upheld the Edmunds Act, and territorial officers began systematic arrest and prosecution of polygamists. There were 1004 convictions for unlawful cohabitation and 31 for polygamy between 1884-93.[12] As the arrests proceeded, it became increasingly hard to prove unlawful cohabitation, and the law was gradually redefined by the local courts until simple refusal to deny the existence of a plural marriage became grounds for imprisonment. These charges of unlawful cohabitation were especially galling to the Mormons, since they were brought only against L.D.S. Church members. Savage mirrored the feelings of many of his neighbors when he exclaimed: "Judge Jones' rulings on cohabitation are only leveled at those who are married, and sustain their wives as such, although he could keep them as mistresses."[13] As

part of the church's effort to deflect prosecution under these stringent laws, lists were made of prominent Washington citizens, including congressmen, who were guilty of cohabitation. The systematic arrests of those suspected of polygamy in Utah continued, however.

Many of Charles' friends were "sent to the Pen" for unlawful cohabitation, and Savage himself at one point worried that he was in danger of being arrested. He expressed this fear in his journal (January 16, 1886) while carefully avoiding any incriminating statements: "I receive an intimation that the minions of the law have my name as an object."

Ironically, although Charles was never arrested for polygamy, he was appointed to visit the Utah Territorial Prison in Sugarhouse, where most of the polygamists were imprisoned. He and several companions were assigned to preach to the prisoners, but prison officials would not allow them to "speak to or recognize anyone." He did manage to bring reading material in to some of the inmates,[14] a welcome relief from the tedium of prison life. "The brethren were dressed in the striped costume of prison rules," he observed. "The murderers, burglars, and horse thieves were all alike. The men of honor and social standing such as encompass the brethren were all on a par with them as far as appearances go."[15]

Many church leaders and other polygamists, refusing to abandon their wives and children, went underground. George Q. Cannon, counselor to L.D.S. President John Taylor, was hounded because of his prominence, and seldom spent two nights in the same place. He was captured in February 1886 en route to Mexico. On his return to Salt Lake City he escaped, was recaptured and released on $45,000 bail, but jumped bail and fled to Arizona. After helping to put church affairs in order, he surrendered to federal officers and served nine months in the Utah Penitentiary.

During Cannon's imprisonment, Charles made several more trips to the Utah Penitentiary, once in company with the Mormon Tabernacle Choir.[16] During these visits he took photographs of the "inside and exterior" of the prison and of the polygamists in their striped prison garb, including Cannon, who sat for a group portrait with a number of other polygamists (fig. 73). Many images in this format were taken, with different men surrounding Elder Cannon in each version, apparently in order to give many people an opportunity to have their picture taken with the influential church leader.[17]

Realizing that the Mormons would not relinquish polygamy even under the stringent provisions of the Edmunds Act, Congress enacted the Edmunds-Tucker Act in February 1887. This was an amendment to the 1862 Morrill Anti-Bigamy law. With this new law the corporation of the L.D.S. Church was dissolved and all property in excess of $50,000 was forfeit to the United States. The Perpetual Emigration Fund, long used to bring immigrants to Utah to bolster the church's political base, was abolished and its assets seized. All church records were opened for inspection, making it easier to prosecute polygamists and seize church property previously protected by proxy owners. The act also abolished women's suffrage in Utah, disinherited children of plural marriages, prescribed a "test oath" to eliminate polygamists from voting, holding public office, or serving on juries, and vested all judicial, law enforcement, and militia powers in the Utah Commission. All marriages were to be certified in the probate courts, and

schools were placed under the direct control of the Territorial Supreme Court. The law also dissolved the Nauvoo Legion and wiped out all existing voting districts.

This new law was clearly unconstitutional in the eyes of the Utah denizens, who promptly provided a test case. While waiting for the results of this test case in the courts, Charles was sent to the East to lobby for relief from the restrictive provisions of the Edmunds-Tucker Act. He was probably chosen for this task because of his national renown, his skills in public speaking, and his many friends and business associates throughout the eastern states. Notwithstanding these assets, he worried about his chances for success. "Start for the states today," he wrote, "to do anything I can against the enforcement of the vile bill to disenfranchise the people of Utah. I feel myself weaker than ever. . . . What can I do is my question? My cause is just—my power very limited."[18]

Charles visited many old friends and business acquaintances on this trip, which took him to Chicago, Boston, and New York. A number of his friends were willing to listen to his views, and he found "many willing to work in our interests."[19]

Despite the support rallied by Charles in the eastern cities, the tidal wave of opposition had grown too strong to withstand. On May 19, 1890, the Supreme Court declared the Edmunds-Tucker Act constitutional. Having lost in the final court of appeals, and faced with total annihilation of their church, L.D.S. President Woodruff and the other leaders of the church issued the "Manifesto." This declaration, sustained by the membership of the church, officially ended Mormon polygamy. After a long and tortuous process, what was left of the seized

FIGURE 75.
Ralph Savage, son of C. R. Savage. Cabinet card by C. R. Savage, c. 1880s. From Savage family photo album.

property was returned to church control.

As heavy a burden as polygamy had been, it proved almost as difficult for many Mormons to discard the principle as it had been originally to embrace it. When the Manifesto was first presented to the body of the church, Charles, along with other members, felt confused and betrayed:

> The authorities maintain that the revelation of God caused them to relinquish the practice of polygamy. Queer times. Can God not foresee the issue of such a movement? And cannot he overrule all things for his plans? i.e. if we have not abused our privileges. I am looking for an instance in the history of the former day Saints where they renounced a part of their faith. Suppose we are asked to renounce any other part of our faith, will we do it? To stop all marriages may be right, to renounce the principle will be wrong.[20]

This assessment proved correct. Although the church agreed to stop the actual practice of plural marriage, polygamy as a principle was never renounced. Some of the more heavily persecuted Saints moved to Canada or Mexico rather than disown their wives and children. Most, like Charles, simply continued to quietly live in polygamy, tacitly ignored by the authorities. No new plural marriages were performed, but few if any existing marriages were dissolved.

The abolition of polygamy enabled Utah to attain the long-awaited status of statehood in 1896. This action removed from Utah the hated federally-appointed governors, judges, and attorneys that had plagued the Mormons for so many years. As part of the negotiations for statehood, Mormon leaders agreed to dissolve the church-backed Peoples Party, and all L.D.S. members were arbitrarily assigned to either the Republican or Democratic parties. Charles was assigned to the Democratic Party.

Not all of the members of the Savage household came by way of polygamy. In addition to his eleven children from two wives, Charles supported several of his in-laws. Annie's mother had died in England, not many years after her departure. All three of Annie's brothers emigrated to America and stayed from time to time with the Savages. After the death of his wife, Annie's father, Robert Adkins, moved to Utah to join his children. He lived with Charles and Annie for many years, until his death in 1888. It is ironic that Hannah, who yearned so fervently to emigrate, never joined the Saints in Utah, while her husband, who never joined the Mormon church, lies buried in his wife's "Promised Land." Unlike Charles, who apparently assimilated quickly into American society, Robert Adkins remained proudly British all his life. In addition to his scorn for their American slang, his grandchildren remembered his proud observance of English holidays, including Guy Fawkes Day. On this day each year he would arm each of the grandchildren with a stick and a pan, and together they would chant:

> Remember, remember, the 5th of November, with gunpowder, treason, and plot. I see no reason why gunpowder treason should ever be forgot. A tupenny's worth to swear him, and good old faggots to burn him; burn his body from his head, then we'll say Old Guy Fawkes' dead, Hurrah!

All would yell "Hurrah!" and beat as loudly as possible on their pans, which delighted the

FIGURE 76.
Robert Adkins, Savage's father-in-law, with two of Savage's children. Albumen print by C. R. Savage, c. 1880. From Savage Book of Remembrance.

THE SAVAGE VIEW

old gentleman.

Annie's brother Thomas lived for years in the Savage household until his early death of a liver abscess in 1874.[21] He died within a few hours of the birth of Annie's ninth child, Ida May Savage. Annie's brother Robert went to Alaska to prospect for gold, and was never heard of again. James Adkins settled in California, where he served as a tutor to a single family for three generations. None of the three brothers ever married.

Savage's own sister Ann had died scarcely two years after his departure from England, and his mother had passed away even before he left for America.[22] His brother George became very well known in the Southampton area for his participation in the local branches of such fraternal organizations as the Foresters and the Oddfellows. A daughter of George Savage, along with her husband, Will Hyde, and their two sons, were later converted to the L.D.S. Church by Charle's son, Ralph, while he was serving a mission in England. They emigrated to Utah, and stayed with the Savage family for at least a short while.[23] James Savage, the youngest brother, has left no trace other than his name and birthdate. Charles did correspond occasionally with his father, despite the family tradition that he had been disowned for joining the Mormon Church. Perhaps his father's attitude softened with time, since after his arrival in Salt Lake City Charles apparently sent him a photograph of his wife Annie. The inscription on the picture states: "This portrait of my wife is affectionately submitted to my father by his son, C. R. Savage."[24]

In 1879, Charles traveled to England and probably visited his two brothers and their families (his father had passed away two years previously). Before leaving Utah, he was appointed as a missionary to "preach the Gospel in Europe," and carried papers with him to that effect. Charles left New York for England on the steam ship "Wyoming," in company with his old friend and partner, George Ottinger, and found life aboard the steamship far more pleasant on this trip than on his original passage across the Atlantic. At one point, however, the ship encountered enough foul weather to cause him to remark that it "seemed like old times." This mission, Savage's third such assignment, was very short, and he spent only two months in England, visiting Manchester, London, Portsmouth, and several other cities. His time was mostly taken up with speaking engagements in the various branches of the L.D.S. Church, but the two men nevertheless found time to go sightseeing in the London area. Savage took photographs of the sights while Ottinger sketched and studied European art.[25] Charles also recorded in his journal several birthdates found in the family Bible.

At the conclusion of Savage's business in England, the Utah artists returned home on the steamship "Montana." Here again, the accommodations were excellent, and a look at the ship's menu reveals almost luxurious fare.[26] Despite these pleasant surroundings, Charles was happy to return to his beloved Utah, and the companionship of his family and friends.

In the late 1860s, Annie had gradually developed progressive hearing loss. She had seen several doctors, and had been told that the quinine she had taken in great quantities to treat her malaria in Council Bluffs was to blame for the deafness. She was the First Counselor in the 20th Ward Relief Society Presidency at that time, and soon afterwards was assigned as President of the Relief Society in her ward. Her

FIGURE 77.
Ship's menu for steamship passage taken by C. R. Savage and Ottinger in 1879. Savage Book of Remembrance.

FIGURE 78.
Annie Adkins Savage. Carte-de-visite by C. R. Savage
with inscription to his father, c. 1861.

sisters in the Relief Society knew of her discouragement from this deafness, and as a token of support and sympathy presented Annie with a wreath of flowers braided from their own hair, which Charles framed for her.[27] Annie became quite proficient in reading lips, and continued her active life of church service and family duties. In later years her son Roscoe was afflicted with a similar disorder, which was eventually discovered to be a hereditary form of deafness.[28]

By the early 1880s Charles held a prominent position in Salt Lake City as both a photographer and a local leader. His photographic views were widely distributed throughout the nation, and were used by many lecturers in their talks and speeches about Utah. One such speaker was Artemus Ward, who used a series of Savage photos in his humorous lantern-slide lectures on Utah and the Mormons.[29] Ward traveled throughout the eastern United States with this presentation for a number of years. He also published newspaper articles using some of these photos.

Savage's stock of glass-plate negatives covered Utah scenery since the early days of the Territory, and enabled him to satisfy the demands of nearly any customer. This supply of negatives was continually being augmented by his frequent excursions into the field. After years of work he had reached a level of financial prosperity. In addition to building a business that could support his extended family, he had created a local industry that employed some of his neighbors and friends. Besides providing work for some, many of his neighbors depended on the few dollars a week Charles was able to give them from the cash register in the Art Bazar. One of Savage's grandsons remembered many such donations,[30] and countless poorer families were helped in this way over the years. Employees of the Art Bazar remember him as a kind and fair employer in an era when employee benefits were meager. When one of his employees fell sick from cancer and could no longer work, he continued to pay her wages, supporting her for two and one-half years until her death.[31] Such treatment earned him the respect and loyalty of his staff, and employment at the gallery was always sought after.

On the evening of Tuesday, June 26, 1883, Charles gathered his family around him at home. Standing on a chair on the back porch, he waved a handkerchief in the air and shouted: "Hurrah, hurrah, hurrah, we're out of debt." The family had a joyful family party to celebrate their freedom from debt after years of struggle, and went to bed tired but happy.[32] Just after midnight, Charles was awakened from sleep and told that his studio was on fire. A neighboring business had caught fire and the flames quickly spread to engulf the Art Bazar. The newspaper account printed the following morning gives a quaint and detailed description of the fire:

A DESTRUCTIVE FIRE, SALT LAKE
CITY VISITED BY A CALAMITY

About ten minutes after midnight this morning flames were seen to suddenly burst out on the premises of Mr. H. B. Clawson, adjacent to the Council House, at the corner of East and South Temple Streets. The alarm was given and the Fire Brigade, with all their apparatus, were speedily on the spot and got a couple of streams on the fire as quickly as possible. Walker Bros. Fire Company and that composed of the employees of the Utah Central Railroad were also soon on the ground, and all worked energetically to extinguish the blaze.

There being a large number of sheds on Mr. Clawson's premises, and the wagons and machinery being largely of an inflammable character, the flames spread with great rapidity, catching the Council House at an early stage, and communicating to Savage's Art Gallery and Sorenson & Carlquist's furniture store.

AN EXPLOSION

Unfortunately Mr. Clawson had stored in an iron cart, or moveable magazine, a quantity of powder. It was located near the gate, at the northwest corner of the grounds, and it appears that no one happened to think of the necessity of wheeling it out on to the street, but when the flames surrounded and the roof of the shed fell in upon it, its danger became apparent to some parties, who shouted to the crowds of people who gathered around to run, as an explosion was inevitable. The warning came none too early, as it occurred almost immediately afterwards, causing a succession of terrific reports that were heard all over town and created general alarm among the citizens, causing thousands who were asleep to awake startled from their slumbers.

When the explosion occurred the sight was grand beyond description. A great mass of flame and burning materials shot high into the air, illuminating the country around for many miles, throwing firebrands in every direction, which fell upon the roofs of buildings, placing them in imminent jeopardy.

The explosion was followed by a crash of glass, the windows of nearly every building within the distance of a block or more, being shivered to atoms. By the concussion, the

west ends of Savage's Art Gallery and Sorenson & Carlquist's furniture store partially gave way and a portion fell in. Attorney Whittemore, who was removing goods from Mr. Savage's came near being buried in the debris. Mr. Harry World, Mr. Dozler, Mr. Farlow and Mr. F. Dunford were in the same building working to save property. The sash and glass of a show window fell upon Mr. Dozler, who received a terrible gash in the head and neck, from which the blood flowed in a copious stream. The writer noted the time when the explosion occurred, being then just half past twelve, nearly twenty minutes after the fire began.

FURTHER SPREAD OF THE FLAMES

By this time the Council House was in a mass of flame, the loss of that building with the exception of the solid stone walls being a certainty. With nearly all its contents, furni-

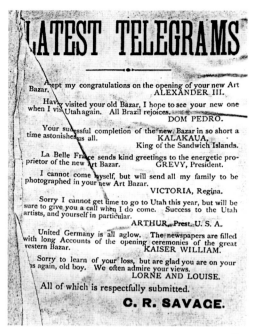

LATEST TELEGRAMS

Accept my congratulations on the opening of your new Art Bazar.
ALEXANDER III.

Have visited your old Bazar, I hope to see your new one when I visit Utah again. All Brazil rejoices.
DOM PEDRO.

Your successful completion of the new Bazar in so short a time astonishes us all.
KALAKAUA,
King of the Sandwich Islands.

La Belle France sends kind greetings to the energetic proprietor of the new Art Bazar.
GREVY, President.

I cannot come myself, but will send all my family to be photographed in your new Art Bazar.
VICTORIA, Regina.

Sorry I cannot get time to go to Utah this year, but will be sure to give you a call when I do come. Success to the Utah artists, and yourself in particular.
ARTHUR, Prest. U. S. A.

United Germany is all aglow. The newspapers are filled with long Accounts of the opening ceremonies of the great western Bazar.
KAISER WILLIAM.

Sorry to learn of your loss, but are glad you are on your is again, old boy. We often admire your views.
LORNE AND LOUISE.

All of which is respectfully submitted.
C. R. SAVAGE.

FIGURE 80.
Art Bazar advertising sheet listing telegrams from around the world, c. 1883. From the Savage Scrapbook.

ture, and appurtenances, including the *Women's Exponent office*, it was entirely consumed with the exception of the outside or shell. The art gallery was completely destroyed. The buildings of the Excelsior bakery and the small shoe shop occupied by Mr. Rawlings were also damaged so as to be rendered useless. The furniture shops of Sorenson & Carlquist and the premises of Mr. Elias Morris and nearly the whole of their contents were a total loss, while the building occupied by Mr. J. H. Parry and his stock of goods, especially books, were badly damaged. In fact, the building, which is a small one, will not be used again. . . .

We understand that Mr. Dozler, who was in the rear of the Art Gallery at the time of the explosion, was knocked over and besides having his face and head cut, received a severe injury in his back and is to-day unable to walk in consequence. . . .

THE ORIGIN, ETC.

The origin of the fire is shrouded in mystery, the general impression being that it was started by an incendiary. No fire was kept in Mr. Clawson's building, and the theory of malicious intent is the most feasible one. It is one of the most destructive fires that has occurred in the history of this city, there having been but one more so, in our recollection—that of the burning of the National Bank building erected by Warren Hussey, which occurred on November 16th, 1875, and involved a loss of $200,000.

Much sympathy is felt for the parties who are the heaviest losers by this calamity, and it is to be hoped that this generous sentiment will take a substantial turn.

(*Deseret Evening News*, June 27, 1883)

When the smoke cleared the following morning, nothing remained of the Art Bazar but rubble. A small portion of the photo supplies had been salvaged by the men working before the explosion, but the great majority had been lost. Aside from the expensive equipment and furnishings within the building, most of his stock of books and other articles for sale was lost. More heartbreaking still was the loss of his irreplaceable glass-plate negative collection, the source of much of his income as well as a valuable historical record. This collection of 12,000 negatives had taken Charles fifteen years to accumulate, through travels of more than 50,000 miles.[33] Of the entire collection, only a single negative survived—the last known photograph of Brigham Young.[34] All the rest were lost: the classic image of the joining of the rails at Promontory, the pictures of Mormon wagon trains on the prairie in 1866, the portraits of prominent local men and women—all these were now preserved only in existing albumen prints. The loss of these negatives accounts for the relative scarcity of some of Savage's images in later years. He recovered his journal from the rubble, and in the charred, water-damaged book he stated quietly: "Store destroyed by fire— twelve years of hard work went up in smoke."

Charles estimated the damages at $12,000 in addition to the loss of the negatives. An insurance policy covered only $4,000 of this amount, but he was determined to start again. Even at the scene of the fire, the Walker brothers from the local bank offered him an interest-free loan to help him rebuild. Some time before this, Savage had suggested to his fellow members of the Mormon Tabernacle Choir that they establish an emergency fund to help any member of the choir who was in need. Ironically, he was the first one benefitted by this plan: the choir held a concert and raised $500 to help rebuild the studio. Many others came forward to donate funds as well. The great support generated in the community to aid Savage demonstrates the high esteem in which he was held. A sizeable portion of his insurance money went to clear his debt with the Anthony Brothers. "This produces but $2,600 in all my insurance money," wrote Charles, "but ends the suit that has lasted nine years. . . . Thank God, the affair is wound up and a thing of the past."[35]

He borrowed the rest of the needed capital, and within six months was at work in a new gallery. Figure 81 shows the new Art Bazar, taken in the mid 1880s. This picture shows the temple nearing completion, and the burned-out shell of the Council House on the corner.

At the opening of the new Art Bazar, the photographer distributed flyers with the "Latest Telegrams" from leaders all over the world, praising the new gallery (fig. 80). It is true that many prominent men had visited the Art Bazar over the years, and that world leaders and many U.S. presidents had visited the western United States in previous years. Charles had even at one point provided a panoramic view of Salt Lake City for Napoleon III.[36] In 1876, the Emperor Dom Pedro of Brazil had visited Salt Lake City, and stopped at the Savage Art Bazar to buy "a large quantity of views of various kinds."[37] It is, therefore, possible that these were actual telegrams, although it is equally likely that this flyer was one of his jokes, a tongue-in-cheek advertising campaign only.

As another advertising ploy, Charles began publishing a four-page newspaper called *The Busy Bee*. This was an expanded version of a small newsletter initially published through the Art Bazar, entitled *Sad Keel's Profetic Messenger* for 1882. *The Busy Bee* was published "spasmodically" for several years,[38] and contained short articles and quotes. The newspaper not only advertised the wares of the Art Bazar, but also promoted other local businesses. The articles and statistics quoted in the paper show that Charles was a strong supporter of locally produced items, and reflect a great pride in Utah and its accomplishments. He included an occasional article on the treatment of certain common diseases, such as diphtheria and erysipelas, for Charles was a proponent of patent medicines and home cures. Among the more unusual cures were breathing the smoke of burning turpentine for diphtheria, and electrical shock treatment for neuralgia or skin diseases. Savage also had great confidence in the curative properties of hyposulfite of soda, the solution also known as fixer, which was used to "fix," or render permanent a photographic image. He recommended that this solution be taken internally to treat erysipelas, poison oak exposure, and other diseases.[39]

After the first issue of *The Busy Bee* was published, the *Ogden Herald* carried a short article announcing the new paper, and included a friendly ribbing of Charles:

Our friend "Charlemagne" is again Savage. He now enters the literary field with laudable ambition, we hope. *The Deseret News* says that, "The BUSY BEE is the title of a little journal, the first number of which is just out. It is dedicated to the workers in the human hive of Deseret and elsewhere, and will be published gratuitously and occasionally by C. R. Savage." If there is a busier bee than Charles, we would like to see him, though we would not like to feel the

FIGURE 81.
Savage's new Art Bazar. Photograph by C. R. Savage, c. 1885. Collection of Bradley Richards.

FIGURE 82.
Cover of Volume 1 of The Busy Bee.
In the Savage Scrapbook.

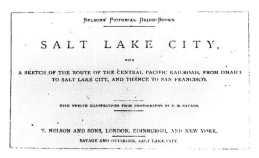

FIGURE 83.
*Title page of Nelson's Pictorial Guide Book
which used Savage photographs for illustrations.
Collection of Utah State Historical Society.*

stings of the *Savage Chawl's.*

Charles quoted this statement in his next issue, and added an equally good-natured reply that "the bees represented by our paper know their friends; their stings are reserved for their enemies."[40]

Soon his business was as active as ever. He set to work repeating many of his original trips, retaking the photographs that had made him famous. These later pictures show an increased appreciation for composition and lighting, demonstrating the years of experience gained since the original photos were taken. His free passes on the railroad allowed him to cover the territory more quickly than on his initial trips. But even more time-saving were the new dry photographic plates that he began using in 1883, which allowed pictures to be taken in the field and developed later, much like modern photographic film. This permitted photographers to take many pictures while the lighting was good, without having to stop after each exposure to develop the plate. The dry plate had existed since the 1860s, but due to the unpredictable nature of the early dry plates, they were not widely used until the 1880s.

When Charles decided to try the dry plates in early 1883, he visited an old friend in California, John Todd. Todd was a Sacramento photographer and part-time hotel owner who taught the Mormon cameraman the principles of dry-plate photography.[41] Charles found it hard work to rebuild his negative collection, but with the aid of the dry plate forged ahead. "The dry plate is a great savings of time and labor," Savage exclaimed. "I am learning photography *de nouveau.*"[42]

Charles used many of these newly re-taken views as illustrations in his ever-expanding line of booklets, pamphlets, and stereoscopic view series. Publications such as his "Reflex of Salt Lake City and Vicinity," "Salt Lake City and the Way Thither," "Views of Utah and Tourist's Guide . . . ," and other pictorial booklets were frequently revised and reprinted. Most of the western railroads continued to publish advertising and informational brochures using photos from the Art Bazar. Savage's "Views of the Great West" were sold as stereoscopic series and postcards across the United States and internationally. He also continued the practice of sending his photos to the illustrated weekly newspapers and journals. He submitted photos to *Harper's Weekly* until around 1870. After that he generally sent images to *Leslie's Illustrated Weekly* instead, possibly because Andrew Russell, his old friend from Promontory days, worked for *Leslie's* as a staff photographer. Other newspapers also used his photographs, often without his permission or credit. Within a year of Savage's arrival in Salt Lake City in 1860, the *Illustrated London News* printed engravings of Brigham Young and his residence, stating that they were taken "from photographs taken recently by C. R. Savage, late of Southampton, and were brought from Salt Lake City by a gentleman who spent several days there early in September."[43] In another instance, Savage pictures were used without credit in a strongly anti-Mormon article entitled, "The Mormons and Their Religion."[44] It is unlikely that this article, published in *Scribner's Monthly*, was illustrated with the permission of the staunch L.D.S. artist.

Charles continued to be actively involved with the professional journals as well, sending pictures to *Humphrey's Journal of Photography* and *The Philadelphia Photographer* from time to time. These were usually listed in the "Editor's Table" or "Correspondence" sections, and provided nation-wide publicity. He also continued to write letters to these journals and to a new journal, *The Photographic Times*, on a variety of photographic subjects. Letters such as "How to be successful as a Photographer," or describing a method of burning celluloid rather than magnesium to make "nocturnal photographs" began to appear in this journal over the next few decades.[45]

With his studio rebuilt and his negative supply again growing, Charles began turning more of the daily operation of the Art Bazar over to two of his sons, Ralph and George, and devoting more time to charitable work in the Salt Lake community. This work, especially among the aged, brought him perhaps even more lasting acclaim than his photographs.

NOTES

1. Savage to Annie Adkins, undated, copy in Savage Book of Remembrance.
2. Savage Journals, July 9-15, 1881.
3. Ellen Fenn was born November 14, 1843, in Billington, Bedfordshire, England.
4. Ellen Fenn and Charles Savage were married October 19, 1878, in the Endowment House, Salt Lake City, by Joseph F. Smith.
5. Benion.
6. Arrington, 238.
7. Arrington, 238.
8. The Relief Society of the L.D.S. Church is today a worldwide organization, and claims the largest membership of any women's organization in the world.
9. Arrington, 357.
10. Arrington, 359.
11. Savage Journals, March 24-25, 1883.
12. Arrington, 360.
13. Savage Journals, April 28, 1885.
14. W. G. Brakely to his wife, July 18, 1886, in Kate B. Carter, Vol. 12.
15. Savage Journals, December 6, 1885.
16. Savage Journals, May 30, June 17, 1887.
17. Examples of these different photographs in the author's possession.
18. Savage Journals, May 15-16, 1890.
19. Savage Journals, May 28, 1890.
20. Savage Journals, November 10, 1891.
21. Savage Journals, January 5, 1874.
22. Savage's sister, Ann Savage, died January 8, 1857, and his mother died October 24, 1852, in Southampton, Hampshire, England.
23. Savage Journals, July 29, August 30, and September 8, 1893.
24. The photograph is in the possession of Harrison Brothers, Savage's grandson. How and why it was returned to Charles from his father, or even whether it was ever sent is uncertain. It is a very early picture of Annie, probably taken soon after her arrival in the Salt Lake Valley.
25. See article on the life of George Ottinger in *Deseret Evening News*, January 22, 1916.
26. Copy of the ship's menu for the "Montana," October 10, 1879, in Savage Book of Remembrance.
27. The braiding of flowers and other ornate designs out of human hair was a common art form throughout Victorian England and the United States. This wreath is now on display with similar articles in the Museum of the Daughters of the Utah Pioneers, in Salt Lake City, Utah.
28. Benion.
29. Browne, 354.
30. Brothers.
31. Savage Journals, June 4, 1890.
32. Clark, *Life Sketch of Charles Roscoe Savage*. The debt to Anthony's was still unresolved.
33. *Deseret Evening News*, June 27, 1883.
34. *The City of the Saints*.
35. Savage Journals, October 18, 1884.
36. *Salt Lake Daily Telegraph*, May 28, 1865.
37. *Deseret News*, April 25, 1876.
38. *The Busy Bee*, 1:5.
39. *The Busy Bee*, 1:2, date unknown; Savage Journals, March 14, 1890.
40. *The Busy Bee*, 1:2, p. 3.
41. Savage Journals, March 24, 1883.
42. Savage Journals, April 30, 1883.
43. "Brigham Young—Brigham Young's Residence," 502.
44. "The Mormons and Their Religion," *Scribner's Monthly* 396-408.
45. Savage, "Notes and news: Nocturnal Photography," 143. At one point Savage took photographs of the interior of Timpanogos Cave in Utah; cave photography was a difficult feat that was rarely attempted in that era. See Bullington's "Timpanogos: The National Parks Mini-Cave."

CHAPTER 8

Hoary-Headed Saints

EDWARD Hunter, presiding bishop of the L.D.S. Church, was sitting in his Salt Lake City office one day in 1874 when he was told that Savage wished to see him. Bishop Hunter asked Charles, who was an old friend, to come in. The forty-two-year-old photographer presented a plan to Bishop Hunter that, although modest enough in its inception, eventually created a major Utah tradition. His plan was to institute an "Old Folks Day," an annual holiday giving the elderly in the community an outing at no expense, to brighten the lives of those who would otherwise remain homebound.[1]

There are several accounts of how Savage conceived the idea for the Old Folks Day. His concern for the poor and elderly was longstanding. As a young man in Utah he had often arranged with local merchants and coal suppliers to provide goods at reduced prices to widows and orphans. He or his friends often paid the remaining cost for the goods, which were usually delivered anonymously, and many tons of coal and groceries were provided to the poor and unfortunate in this manner. The bulk of the produce from the Savage family garden found its way into the homes of elderly neighbors as well. A granddaughter of Savage recalls that each year when the sweet peas ripened, Charles and Annie would have a "Pea Festival," where elderly neighbors were brought to their home for a dinner, featuring the newly-picked peas.[2] This was said to have grown larger each year, until finally he decided to organize it into a city-wide project.

Other authors have stated that, while attending social activities in Salt Lake City, "[Savage] noticed that the old fathers and mothers, especially the mothers, usually were engaged in tending their grandchildren, while the younger parents enjoyed themselves in the dance. Taking in this situation the idea of an Old Folks Day in which the aged might be waited upon by the younger generation and at least on one day of the year be treated as special guests of honor occurred to Mr. Savage."[3]

One of Savage's daughters related a different story of the beginning of the Old Folks Day. According to her, Charles frequently passed the home of his neighbor, John Daynes, and whenever he went by, "he would see John's elderly mother sitting on the porch. She was there day after day, year after year, whenever the weather would permit, and Savage wondered if she ever went outside of the yard. He thought that there must be other old people that lived in the same way."[4]

Whatever prompted the idea, it eventually led to that meeting in Bishop Hunter's office. The Old Folks Day, as outlined by Savage, would be open to men and women of all religions, races and creeds, the only condition for their participation being "that they must have reached a certain mile-post in life's highway." In practical application, this meant seventy years old or more. The activity was to be provided without charge, and supported by donations from local merchants and individuals.

Bishop Hunter was delighted with the suggestion, and assigned his secretary, George

FIGURE 84. (OPPOSITE)
"Watching the results of the cake walk,"
Old Folks Day, Lagoon, July 6, 1898. Albumen print
by C. R. Savage. Collection of the Utah State
Historical Society.

FIGURE 84.
Old Folks Day excursion ticket, 1899.
From Savage Scrapbook.

Goddard, a close friend of Charles, to assist him. The two men set to work to make the necessary arrangements. Charles arranged with the Utah Western Railroad and the local streetcar company to provide transportation for the event. On May 14 of that same year, 180 elderly men and women, with 60 attendants, went by rail to Lake Point, on the south shore of the Great Salt Lake. A program was held at the hotel run by Dr. Clinton, and the guests were royally entertained. After refreshments were served, many of the guests boarded the steamer "City of Corinne," and had a pleasant two-hour trip on the Great Salt Lake. After more refreshments, music and dancing were provided at the Clinton Hotel, and the aged excursionists taken back to the city by rail. A delightful time was had by all participants, and the decision was made to continue the custom as an annual event.

The idea of Old Folks Day spread quickly to other Utah communities, and became the custom in almost every town of consequence in the Territory. Often, out-of-town trips were made, when Old Folks from several communities were entertained by the citizens of another community, who acted as hosts. The host city varied, this post being filled by Ogden, Provo, American Fork, Springville, Brigham, Payson, Pleasant Grove, Tooele, and Salt Lake City. Often the excursions were held at resorts, some of the favorites over the years including Garfield Beach, Black Rock, Saltair, Lagoon, and Wandemere and Liberty parks in Salt Lake City.

Over time, the gatherings became more widely attended and better funded, but Charles Savage and George Goddard always remained the appointed committee heads to organize the festivities. Savage's association with the various western railroads was invaluable, and railroad

officials donated free passage to participants of the Old Folks Day on many occasions. The elderly passenger's "ticket" for the train ride was a ribbon badge worn on the left breast. Seventy-year-old participants wore a red badge, blue badges represented those past eighty, while a white badge was worn by those few who had made it into their nineties.[5]

During L.D.S. President John Taylor's administration, the church donated one hundred dollars to the Old Folks Committee each year. Other local merchants donated cash or merchandise to be used either for refreshments or as door prizes for the competitions held each year. These door prizes were awarded for all sorts of achievements, and were usually the subject of great humor. A prize was invariably given to the oldest man or women present. One visitor to the 1882 excursion to Liberty Park observed:

There were a thousand and forty-eight old people over seventy. . . . There were races run by the old men, and prizes given to some. One old lady got a dollar for having a bonnet that was twenty years old and in a good state of preservation. A dollar was given to an old man for getting up and making the fire in the morning for his wife for more than sixty years. . . . Brother William Naylor got a dollar for living peacefully with his mother-in-law for twenty-five years. It seems almost incredible, but he is a man of truth.[6]

An "Old Folks Choir" was organized by Charles and his friend and fellow Mormon Tabernacle Choir member, William H. Foster. This choir began in 1881, and became a favorite part of the program in the many years that it continued. Other singers participated in the program, as did actors and prominent local leaders. Although the excursions were usually arranged for the summer, annual winter activities were also planned for the elderly. Free admission to the Salt Lake Theater, and later to other theaters, was often arranged. Other unfortunates were later provided with similar privileges, and orphans, widows, deaf-mutes, and newsboys were invited to attend these free performances at the Theater.[7]

The Old Folks Day continued as a Utah tradition for ninety-five years, outlasting Charles by more than six decades. Eventually the population of Utah grew too large to successfully carry out this tradition, and in 1970 the Old Folks Day was abandoned as a church-wide activity. The responsibility for honoring the elderly was passed on to local L.D.S. Church leaders.

Years after Savage's death, the Old Folks Committee erected a monument to honor the pivotal role he had played in organizing Old Folks Day in Utah (fig. 85). The monument was "in the nature of a drinking fountain,"[8] and was "constructed of richly veined, red-streaked Stony Creek Granite from Massachusetts. The bronze bust and plaque are especially fine, being the work of Gilbert Riswold who was also the sculptor of the 'Mormon Battalion Monument' on Capitol Hill." The plaque read:

"In affectionate remembrance of Charles R. Savage, and in reverential regard for the old folks whose happiness he so greatly promoted through the establishment of Old Folks Day in Utah."

The monument was placed on the southeast corner of Temple Square, facing the site of the Art Bazar, where it remains today—honoring a man who spent much of his life in the service of his elderly friends.

In addition to Old Folks Day, Charles was involved in many other community activities during the 1890s. He was nominated as the Democratic candidate for the Utah State Senate in 1895, and wrote several editorials to the local papers during this election year.[9] He lost the election, and never again ran for public office, despite repeated requests by friends and associates. Even when not running for election himself, he wrote articles for the papers urging political unity among his fellow Mormons, and promoting issues of a progressive nature. The mandatory two-party political system in Utah had changed with the introduction of the American Party, a group comprised mainly of "Gentiles" (non-Mormons) in Utah, and often referred to by L.D.S. Church members as "the Liberals." Although Mormons were still in the majority in Utah, their vote was usually split between the Democratic and Republican parties, allowing the American Party to garner a majority of votes for many candidates. Charles considered this a travesty, and in a scathing letter to a Salt Lake newspaper wrote the following:

Sorrow fills my heart when I see three parties struggling for the mastery. It reminds one of a picture I once saw illustrating the possession of a cow, each of the litigants was pulling, one at the head, the other at the tail, while the lawyers were milking her. It was so at the last election, it will be so again, if the same policy is pursued.

Allegiance to party seems to blind the eyes of many men, a city on the verge of bankruptcy cannot be saved by such actions, the conditions confronting us require definite

FIGURE 85.
Bronze bust and drinking fountain commemorating Charles Savage. It now stands on the corner of South Temple and Main Streets in Salt Lake City. Press photo taken in 1936.

FIGURE 86.
Electric Light Works, Ogden Canyon, Utah.
Photograph by C. R. Savage.

FIGURE 87.
Detail of figure 86 showing Savage's copyright signature
and title in the negative.

FIGURE 88.
Detail of figure 86, reproduced without permission by
Pratt, Ogden City, Utah. The title and photographer's
credit have been carefully obscured.

action, it is the solemn duty of all taxpayers to see that none but responsible business men control municipal affairs, they are the only ones fit to transact business, men who are successful in the ordinary walks of life.

The vote for city officials last election stood as follows:

Total Republican vote, 7,650.

Total Democratic vote, 4,638.

Total "American" vote, 8,589.

Apply these results to the simile of the cow, and you can guess the result, the last named party taking the place of the lawyer. Stick to the party lines and you hand the city over to the great irresponsibles who have mismanaged its affairs in the most reckless manner.

The only way out is to unite on men of merit, despite their political standing, who are opposed to the present administration.[10]

Other political issues such as women's suffrage, the prohibition of liquor, and the fiscal responsibility of public officers were repeatedly addressed in these years by Charles. These articles, although clearly influenced by his religious perspective, never failed to show Savage's excellent sense of humor. Other articles had a more personal viewpoint. In an article addressed "To the Pirates of Utah (Not of Penzance)," Charles registered a public complaint that many other photographers and printers were using his pictures publicly without giving either credit or royalties.[11] This article may refer to C. W. Carter, Savage's old employee, since he was known to make copies of other photographers' work. No names were mentioned in the article, however. Copyright observance for photographs had improved since the 1860s, but still remained sporadic at best.

Charles was asked on several occasions to write faith-promoting articles for Latter-day Saint publications such as *The Juvenile Instructor*, and the *Improvement Era*.[12] These were usually inspirational essays, written to young people in a Horatio Alger "rags to riches" style. This is not surprising, considering Savage's own rise to national renown from the humblest of beginnings.

The last newspaper article ever penned by Savage was entitled "Plea of C. R. Savage for the Saloon Victims."[13] In addition to its good-natured sarcasm, this piece is typical of Charles' practical attitude toward his life and religion:

I have no use for the saloon; it means trouble wherever you find it. No man was ever known to be proud of running one. There is no argument that can be used in favor of its continuance. It has been called the poor man's club room—the place where he can go on a cold day and get warm. He can always find a welcome there. It is the place where he can meet a friend and often get a free lunch, the consideration being that when he wants a drink he can get supplied by the keeper of the club. In fact, I have seen men stay in the saloon until the time came for closing, and they were then tumbled into the street; in some places I have known the keepers to allow their half-drunken habitues to sleep in the chairs until morning.

The saloon habit has become a serious one for thousands of working men, and what shall be done for these unfortunates when these resorts are closed and prohibition is the law of the state? Where will the homeless bachelor, and the transient go when his day's work is done? Where can he spend his evenings generally, the facilities in cheap rooming houses are very poor and comfortless?

There are no homes in which he will be welcome, there are no public halls where he can read or meet a friend. Possibly he may find a welcome such as the Salvation Army provides.

Instead of feeding and caring for drunks and vagrants at the expense of the city, why cannot we establish a working man's club room, free to the stranger and the homeless transient, under well conducted arrangements. Facilities for bathing and other conveniences could also be obtained there at a low rate. It would be a reading room and a hall of refuge in the long winter evenings.

It is no small thing to break a man of the saloon habit and if we rob him of a chance to fool away his hard earnings, we will have to point out to him a more excellent way. It is the duty of all the citizens who are free from the curse of liquor to lend a helping hand to those less favored than themselves. The way to preach temperance is to help our fellow men to practice it.

Savage's feelings about the use of strong drink were further echoed in his journal entry for the Fourth of July, 1893. A great celebration was held at Saltair, the resort on the shore of the Great Salt Lake. "Nearly everybody went to Saltair," he dryly noted. "It is reported that a thousand cases of beer were drunk by the visitors. What a comment on the rising glory of Zion!"

Because of his involvement in social and political activities, Savage was often asked to participate on committees. In 1897, when Utah celebrated the fiftieth anniversary of the entry of the Mormon pioneers into the Salt Lake valley, Charles was one of ten committee members chosen to organize the celebration.[14] Years earlier, when the great San Francisco earthquake and fire destroyed Southern Pacific Railroad's stock of negatives, pictures, and advertising publications, they turned to Savage for help. When Southern Pacific's official photographer arrived in Salt Lake City, Charles gave him unlimited access to his own negative collection at no charge, so that the railroad could publish a new travel guide.

On another occasion, when a friend's store was destroyed by fire, Charles personally canvassed the city for donations to rebuild the business. The Art Bazar served as the clearing house for this and many other charitable activities in the city over the years. When the L.D.S. Conference sermons centered around self-sufficiency and the exclusive use of home-produced items, Charles publicly announced that one half of his storefront window would be available to advertise any home-produced articles at no charge. On another occasion, when a local store was burned to the ground, the owner was allowed to sell his wares without commission from the Art Bazar until his own store was rebuilt.

As Salt Lake City grew, more photographers set up galleries in the area. More than a few of them were young men originally trained as apprentices and assistants in the Art Bazar. Many later Utah photographers such as George Edward Anderson, James Fennemore, Hiram Sainsbury, and Walter Stringham first learned their trade at the Art Bazar before setting up their own galleries. This led Savage to lament in his journal: "Thus it goes—as soon as any one gets really useful, off they go!" But he loved his apprentices, and often helped them start their own business, despite the increased local competition to his own studio. In his journals and other writings Savage continually expressed pride in his young assistants. Even when, in a rare episode, an employee had to be released because of poor performance, the journal reflected disappointment rather than resentment.

The increased competition for photography led Charles to further expand his business to include many types of retail items. The Valentine's Day trade was one of the first areas into which he ventured. Valentines had traditionally been handmade, but with increasing affluence, Utah citizens wanted to buy ready-made, imported valentines. Charles began producing homemade valentines at a fraction of the cost of the imported ones, and selling them in the store. Most of these were made by his own family members, and were eventually distributed to outlets across the city. This business grew for about ten years, until the price of imported valentines dropped so low that it became unprofitable. By then the Art Bazar had developed a reputation for selling valentines, and continued to sell the imported article profitably.

He also found that he could buy many small wares in the East, such as scissors and needles, and sell them in Utah at a good profit. He began making yearly trips to California and the eastern cities to buy in high volume for the Art Bazar, often accompanied by one of his sons. His free passes on the railroads made this very economical, and his many railroad contacts helped him negotiate cut-rate freight prices that often saved him hundreds of dollars.

Within five years after the fire, Charles had completely recovered from the debts incurred in rebuilding, when a new economic threat appeared on the horizon. Land prices in Utah, previously very stable in this agricultural society, began to rise dramatically. This boom in real estate was due in part to the influx of non-Mormons on the railroads, the development of mining interests, and the expected "overthrow" of the L.D.S. Church after the passage of the Edmunds-Tucker Act. Charles was only leasing the property on which the gallery was built, and with the rising land prices, ran a very real risk of having his place of business sold out from underneath him. He hurriedly arranged to borrow money yet again to buy the land on which the Gallery stood.[15] The real-estate boom lasted only a short while, and land prices again stabilized, but by that time Charles was well on his way to owning the Art Bazar.

Business was brisk in the 1880s and 1890s. The portrait photography trade held steady, and the sale of novelties, toys, art materials, and picture frames grew each year. Christmas and Valentine's Day were busy seasons, as were the semi-annual L.D.S. conferences with their resultant influx of out-of-town visitors. Savage catered to the tourist trade, and was always on the look-out for new souvenirs to sell. Local artisans made souvenirs from trees planted by Brigham Young and sold them in the Art Bazar. Fossils, minerals, and other local oddities were likewise to be found there.

Despite the financial success of his business ventures, Charles did not particularly enjoy the life of a businessman. "Verily business is a trying, taxing effort," he said, "about like trying to float on the ocean on a plank in a gale of wind."[16] He was clearly happiest when pursuing his chosen trade—landscape photography. His love for this work is demonstrated by the sheer volume of beautiful landscape views he produced. His journals also express deep satisfaction in traveling through the wild regions of the inter-mountain West, searching for new views to make. Scarcely a summer passed without at least two or three full-scale viewing trips.

Savage's other great loves were his work with the Old Folks Committee and his service to his church. In 1884 he had been appointed a Home Missionary, with the commission to preach to non-members throughout the Salt Lake area. He faithfully performed this office for many years, and was constantly in demand as a speaker on both religious and secular topics.

In April, 1892, Savage was present to photograph the completion of the exterior of the L.D.S. temple in Salt Lake City. The temple, forty years in the building, had become a monument to the faith and perseverance of the Mormon people. Built of granite from a nearby quarry, all of the work was done by local craftsmen and laborers. Through lean times and good, pioneers had donated time and materials to help build the structure. The final stone of the temple, the capstone, was laid during the April conference of 1892. The completion of the temple fulfilled a sixty-year-old dream for the Mormons, who had seen two previous temples in Ohio and Illinois desecrated and destroyed. It had become a focal point of the Mormon faith, and its completion was viewed as a literal fulfillment of divine prophecy, a sign that the Mormon people had found their Promised Land, their place of rest. Not surprisingly, the April 6 celebration of laying the capstone became an occasion of rich spiritual outpouring for the Utah Saints. In his journal, Savage described his participation in the event as follows:

The Conference which began on the 3rd and closed with the placing of the capstone on the Temple was one of the best of any one that I have attended. The teachings were forcible and dealt with the vital interests of the Church. The most important was the placing by electricity of the top stone under the Angel Moroni—designed by Mr. Dallin. Electric incandescent lamps surround the finials on golden-pointed terminals to each of the gothic pinnacles. The assembly was greater than any one witnessed before in our city. The estimate was that 30,000 persons were on and around the block. When the great song, "The Spirit of God" was sung by the united audience, a feeling different thrilled through me from any one ever experienced. The hosannah shout was something long to be remembered and one I never expect to hear again during my life.

Charles took several views of this assembly, one of which is shown in figure 90. The picture shows the temple still surrounded by its scaffolding. In the left foreground is the Savage Art Bazar. The canopy over the Art Bazar was sturdy enough to walk on, and the picture shows several people on the canopy as well as on the roof of the Art Bazar building. One of Savage's granddaughters noted that family members would often sit on the canopy to get a good view of local parades and other events.[17] In later years, employees of the Savage photographic gallery also enjoyed the privilege of sitting on the canopy, especially in the evenings when local bands would play on the sidewalk below.[18]

Although some authors have suggested that Savage sang with the Mormon Tabernacle Choir during the capstone ceremony and therefore

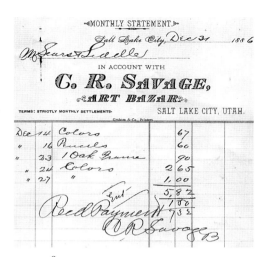

FIGURE 89.
Receipt from C. R. Savage's Art Bazar. Collection of James P. Crain.

FIGURE 90.
*Laying of the capstone, Mormon Temple,
April 6, 1892, mammoth view by C. R. Savage.
Collection of the L.D.S Church Archives.*

could not have taken photographs of the proceedings, his journal entries are very clear on the subject. One month after the ceremony Savage wrote, "My views of the laying of the capstone are meeting with good sale."[19] As a member of the choir, Savage may well have sung during part of the ceremonies, and this might explain why he did not take images from different angles. Certain it is that Savage only took photos from a single vantage point, in contrast to the multiple views taken by other local photographers.[20]

Although the temple structure itself was now complete, it took another year to finish the interior and prepare the temple for dedication. Two days prior to the temple dedication, Charles reported that he took "a picture of the special window in the Sealing room to day—and see the Temple. Most beautiful in Every detail."[21] Charles sang in the choir at the dedication of the Temple, another event of great spiritual meaning for him:

Never in my life did I feel an influence like unto the one I felt during the ceremony. Every heart was touched with the divinity of our surroundings. . . . I never had more great joy than I then felt. My soul was filled with peace and my whole nature replete with satisfaction. The ceremony lasted four hours. The talk was inspiring. The music rendered by 300 members of the Choir was all original and very fine. I never felt nearer to the invisible powers than while in the Temple. I never had a stronger testimony than on this occasion.[22]

Later that same year Charles was again called upon in his capacity as a choir member. The choir was embarking on a tour across the United States, with concerts in Kansas City, St. Louis, New York, Independence, Washington D.C., Omaha, Boston, and Philadelphia. The choir also stopped at Chicago for the World's Fair. The "Columbian Exhibition," as it was touted, had a "Utah Day," during which the choir was featured in concert and displays of the industries and produce of the state were shown.

This was the first real national exposure for the Mormon Tabernacle Choir. In the face of the severe anti-polygamy sentiment of the early 1890s, Utah Day at the World's Fair provided some much-needed publicity for the Territory. The concert tour was the first such trip for the thirty-year-old group, and began a tradition of musical excellence that has grown steadily over the years. The choir took second place in the music competition at the fair. Savage, of course, felt that it should have earned first place.[23]

Charles enjoyed the fair, although he complained in his journal of the "poor arrangements for feeding the people. . . . It is gouge, gouge, gouge everywhere."[24] As usual, he was fascinated by the scientific displays that showed the rising technology of the coming industrial age.

He also entered a selection of his own photographs for competition in the fair. According to his journal, he and William Henry Jackson of Denver were the only U.S. photographers that were "making a show." Charles wistfully observed that the photographs taken by Jackson were "larger and better printed than mine, showing his superior facilities."[25] Despite the competition, he learned months later that he had been awarded a medal and diploma for his photographs.

His return home that year was marred by the sudden death of his first wife Annie. She had suffered from a kidney disease for some time, and on Thanksgiving Day, 1893, her condition suddenly worsened. Charles called in the Mormon Elders to administer to her, and while they were blessing her she died. In his journal, the grief-stricken photographer wrote:

None of us anticipated so sudden a collapse. Everything possible was done to save her, but the time had come for one of the noblest, gentlest companions that ever a man had to separate from her earthly chores. I have suffered the greatest loss I can sustain—and God help me to sustain it properly. The boys and girls acted like heroes and heroines. . . .

Sister Kate Wells and Sister Culmer laid Ma out. After they had done this her face assumed a beautiful expression of satisfaction and peace. Nothing could have been more comforting to us. It said, "My work is done. I have triumphed over death. Peace unto you all."

Annie had long waited to see the Salt Lake Temple completed. Once she took a trip with Ellen, Charles' third wife, to the Logan Temple to do temple ordinances for her mother and other deceased relatives, but returned home disheartened when she found that her hearing problem prevented her from doing the work in the Temple. After that, she fervently hoped to see the Salt Lake Temple finished, for she felt that if she could go through that temple her hearing would be restored. In 1888 Annie had been given a "Patriarchal Blessing" by local church leaders in which she was promised that if she wished, she would be allowed by the Lord to live five more years. Annie did live just five years, long enough to see the new temple dedicated, but died before she could visit it.

Annie's funeral was held in the 20th Ward chapel; no previous funeral had been so well attended. Emily H. Woodmansee, a close friend of Annie's and a renowned local poetess and author, wrote a poem in her honor that was published in a Salt Lake City newspaper.[26] Friends and family gathered round to comfort Charles in his bereavement. As the year closed, the aging cameraman wrote of his loss:

This is the saddest month of my life. I have tried to meet the bereavement like a man. The children have done the same. They all acted well and have continued to do so since Mamma died. Business has fallen off, but I have managed to get enough to pay my debts and on the 30th of the month I was able to pay every dollar I owed. Thanks to God for his mercies. Evidences of kindly feelings entertained for Mamma pour in on every hand. All who knew her loved her. Thus passes away the year most to be remembered in my life.[27]

Charles never again spent a Thanksgiving Day at home, but always arranged to be on a trip or visiting friends during the holiday. As the nineteenth century began to draw to a close, the effects of time began to tell on Savage. Now well into his sixties, with gray hair and beard, he had a stately appearance becoming to a successful businessman and local leader (fig. 91). He was variously described as "stout" or "solid," but never accused of being overweight. A phrenological evaluation published in the *Salt Lake Herald* described him as "a very good specimen of physical manhood, standing 5 feet 10 ½ inches high and weighing 200 pounds. The circumference measurement of his head is 23 ¼ inches and all the other measurements in equal proportion."[28]

Although he continued to help out in the studio, the main responsibility for the business was turned over to his sons, Ralph and George. George managed the art store, while Ralph handled the portrait photography. The elder Savage's business acumen remained a guiding force in the studio, however, and his name and reputation continued to draw business to the Art Bazar.

But the nature of photography had changed again. With the introduction of the dry plate in the 1870s, photography was no longer a difficult art, burdened by complex chemistry and awkward equipment. The amateur photographer was born. With the convenient dry plate, the amateur could go out to take pictures and return home hours later to develop and print the views. Many companies began manufacturing dry plate cameras, and in the 1880s and 1890s they were actively sold through catalogs such as Sears, Roebuck and Co., with beginner's instruction books and all the necessary equipment.

In the 1880s, a young bank clerk named George Eastman went into the business of producing dry photographic plates. By 1888, he had developed the first commercially successful camera using roll film rather than glass plates. This original "Kodak" (a name invented by Eastman to be both distinctive and easy to pronounce) was the beginning of a great expansion in amateur photography. "Nearly everybody is becoming a photographer," sighed Charles. "Business is changing to developing and finishing views for amateurs. The great improvements in reproductive photography have killed wood engraving and kindred arts. Most of the magazines now published are illustrated by photo engravings—the demand for views is gradually falling off."[29]

Savage, however, was enough of an entrepreneur to shift with the changing times. Although he reported that he was "not doing much viewing lately" because of the decreased demand for the work, he turned his attention to other, more lucrative practices. The Art Bazar still carried on a steady trade in art supplies, books, and stationary, and Ralph continued to operate the portrait studio. The framing shop was eventually managed by another of Savage's sons, Rock (Roscoe), after he retired from his railroad job.

The store was expanded to include all sorts of wares, from photographic implements for amateurs to darkroom equipment and chemicals. Lessons in photography were given at the Savage studio as well. Charles arranged for wholesale and retail contracts with the Eastman Kodak Company, and received a percentage of the price of any Kodak products sold in Utah, Idaho, Wyoming, and Montana.[30] He had similar arrangements with other companies, including DeVoe Watercolors, Detzkin, and three different picture frame molding companies. Professional surveying equipment and optical

devices were retailed on the first floor. Stationary, pens, pencils, and cards also sold well, and the upper floor of the Art Bazar carried a complete toy department, with dolls, tricycles, and rocking horses.[31]

All of these enterprises were fairly self-sufficient, and after his gradual retirement from the studio around 1906 Savage was able to spend more time with his family. In addition to his three sons who worked at the studio, a daughter, Nan Savage Richardson, helped out from time to time. Another daughter, Ida May Savage, learned to tint photographs with watercolors, and won several prizes in territorial and state fairs over the years. She also became an accomplished artist in her own right, producing both watercolors and oils. Still another daughter, Lennie Louise Savage Riter, became one of Utah's best known stage actresses.

In 1896, a young graduate of the University of Utah, Joshua Reuben Clark, was "running the light" for Savage in one of his many lectures accompanied by lantern slides.[32] Within eighteen months, J. Reuben Clark, a school teacher in Heber City, married Charles' daughter Luacine. Charles was required to serve on jury duty, and could not attend the ceremony. He was impressed with his new son-in-law, and stated that "he is a very earnest and honest talker, and will be a man of mark someday."[33] After years of working in Washington, D.C., in a high position in the State Department, J. Reuben Clark returned to Utah and eventually served in the First Presidency of the L.D.S. Church.

Charles was first and foremost a family man, and loved to spend time at home with his grandchildren. His family remembered him as being very good with children. There were family outings to Liberty Park and Calder's Park in Salt

FIGURE 91.
Portrait of Charles Savage, c. 1895. Albumen print from Savage Book of Remembrance.

Lake City, and every Christmas he spoiled the grandchildren with gifts. One grand-daughter, Louise Benion, remembered that she was allowed to choose her own birthday present from the Art Bazar:

On one of my birthdays he told me to go down and select a doll from the store. Well, that was one of the biggest thrills of my life! These dolls were in cases on the wall, and I could select one for my birthday. Mother was with me. I don't remember what the first doll I selected was, but I guess it was rather costly, and Mother told me it was a little too much. So I got another one, a lovely French doll, and I remember it cost $4.00, because that doll never had a name, I always called it my 4-dollar doll. I had that doll for years.

The elderly photographer also gave two of his young grandchildren who were visiting from out of town an allowance of ten cents a week. The day that Charles died, he had two dimes in his pocket that he was bringing home for his little granddaughters.

At the age of sixty-three, several years after

his first wife's death, Charles married Annie Smith Clowes (fig. 93).[34] She was a widow, with grown children, and Savage's children and grandchildren called her Aunt Annie. The Savage family accepted her without reserve, since both she and her first husband had been friends of the family for many years, but little else is known about the details of this union or of her life with Charles.

Friends, too, claimed much of the artist's time after retirement. He was often to be found in the company of his very closest friends: George Goddard, William Eddington, George Ottinger, William Dunbar, and Alfred Lambourne. Lambourne, a celebrated poet and author, often called "Utah's Thoreau," had been a traveling companion for years. Charles and his friends often teased one another, and on one occasion, an unknown friend sent a composite picture of Charles to a newspaper, where it was published with the following article:

If anybody has doubts about the above being a very good picture of Charles R. Savage, he is invited to call at the Art Bazar and say so. The consequences will probably be disastrous, because it is said that he "took it" himself. He had assumed the expression desired on the part of his customers when he requests them to "look pleasant, please." Mr. Savage is the ideal of the old folks, having originated the "graft" of making those who can afford it pay for the pleasure of those whose positions in life are such that only occasionally sunbeams cross their path. As a result, he can have the "old folks' vote" for any office to which he might aspire. He has been heard to say, however, that he would rather be found handing out presents to the

FIGURE 92.
Salt Lake City Temple Square.
Photo by Ralph Savage from L.D.S. Church Archives.

old folks on their annual "toots" than be President of the United States. His friends say he would refuse the offer of nomination for the Presidency were it tendered to him, but they fail to say that he was born abroad.

That he is very amiable is shown by the fact that he has taken several long trips with Alfred (Savage calls him "Fred") Lambourne without losing his temper; that he has a keen sense of humor has been shown at other times when he has actually dissected and enjoyed one of the jokes of that same artist-author.

There are thousands who will join in the wishes of the writer, "May his shadow never grow less."
(*Salt Lake Tribune*, February 5, 1908)

Reunions with old acquaintances from the London Conference were organized and attended by Charles. Other community projects filled the hours as well. Photographers in the western states had organized themselves into the Inter-Mountain Photographers Association, and in 1908 Charles offered the use of the Art Bazar to host their convention. The letter advertising the event stated that "there will be capable instructors present who will give demonstrations in lighting and posing under the skylight, also on developing, printing, toning, etc. Mr. C. R. Savage, the pioneer Photographer will give a talk on, what the photographer should know."[35]

Charles continued to lecture on many subjects. He was a member of the Microscopical Society in Utah, and occasionally presented papers with titles like "Wonders of the Mighty Deep" and "Life in Arctic Seas." He took pleasure trips along most of the western railroads, and wrote travelogues that were printed in the

local papers. These were often laced with comparisons of Utah to surrounding states, and he was continually praising the attributes of his own beloved state.

In late January of 1909, Charles went to Ogden to spend the day at the home of a "Brother McCune." After an "enjoyable time," he returned to Salt Lake City.[36] This was his last journal entry. The following Saturday he went in to the Gallery, but complained to his son George of "feeling poorly." At the suggestion of his son, he returned home to rest, but his condition gradually worsened. Just after midnight, February 3, 1909, he died of heart failure at the age of seventy-six.

"C. R. Savage Called by Death" was the headline in the *Deseret Evening News* the next day, "One of the Most Beloved Men in Utah Succumbs to Heart Failure." Other papers joined in to lament the passing of Savage: "The Friend of the Old Folks," "Well-Known Member of Mormon Church," and "Pioneer Photographer." Many were surprised at his sudden passing, since he had enjoyed excellent health until only a few days before his death.

Years earlier, Charles had attended the funeral of an associate, and had been saddened at the poor attendance at the services. As he looked at the meager showing, he had felt that the measure of a man's success in life might well be counted in the number of friends who mourned his passing. If this assessment was any indication, then Savage was, indeed, a successful man. His funeral was held in the Assembly Hall on Temple Square, a structure often photographed by Charles in life. Despite the large size of this building, it was "filled to over-flowing," said the newspapers. "Every seat was occupied, many stood in the hallways, and others

FIGURE 93.
Annie Smith Clowes, C. R. Savage's fourth wife. From Savage Book of Remembrance.

were unable to gain admission." Many local and church leaders participated in the services, including Bishop George Romney, James E. Talmage, John Winder, and Hyrum E. Smith.

Although eulogies may be an unrealistic way to judge a man's character, some of the speakers related stories about the pioneer photographer that clearly demonstrated his love for his fellow men. "He was liberal, and was always planning to help someone," said Bishop Romney. "He so often said: 'we are going to contribute to this or that fund, we are going to help this or that brother.'"

Bishop Nibley stated: "He was honest. He spoke the truth. He dealt considerately. It was his nature to be compassionate. He was a peculiarly sensitive man. . . . He never interfered with the rights of others. Unconsciously he has erected his own monument." Joseph Taylor told of an Old Folks outing taken with Savage. At one point Taylor had said to him, "'Brother Savage, you are immortalizing your name.' [Savage] said, as he put his hand on my shoulder, 'Brother, let my name sink into oblivion. If I can help others, I will be glad.'"

Western railroad men sent their condolences, and also praised the character of the well-known railroad photographer. "C. R. Savage was one of the grandest men I ever knew. . . . No man in the history of railroading in the West was more loved and respected among railroad men than C. R. Savage," said one railroader.[37] "His many little acts of kindness to the railroad men of the West can never be forgotten," wrote another.[38] In a tribute to Savage, John P. Meakin wrote: "He was the loving peasant prince of Utah, so dear to our hearts that, though seventy-seven years of age, we called him 'Charley.'" Another tribute to Charles was penned by his long-time friend, artist Alfred Lambourne, who reminisced about the many travels taken with his dear friend:

C. R. Savage was a lover of nature. He loved nature more than art. Next to mankind, he loved the solitude, the prairie, the forest, the mountains, and the sea. How often it happened that we passed a Sabbath day together, that upon that day we looked at the beauties of untouched nature. Sabbaths that left an indelible imprint upon heart and brain. . . .

But other Sabbaths we passed together; beneath the marvelous cliffs of Yosemite, amid the shadowy solitude of the Mariposa Grove, by the thundering waters of the Shoshone, by the Columbia River, looking on the snow-covered cones of Mt. Hood and Mt. Shasta, upon the expanse of cactus and sand of the Gila Desert, amid the wonders of the Yellowstone Canyon, by the great mural fronts of the temples of the Rio Virgin and by those walls between which, in its deep sunk bed, flows the Colorado. . . .

It was not exactly that my friend looked upon nature with the artist's worship, or lust of the eye, or with the adoration and dreaming of the poet. There was something in his love of nature which was practical, robust and yet affectionate. Then it was that one learned to know the man, to know all that was best and deepest in his friendship, to see beneath the surface, to know what guided the main currents of his life. Then one learned of his almost child-like simplicity and his love for that which was good and true.[39]

So ended the career of Charles Roscoe Savage, pioneer photographer. His photographic work covered a period of half a century, from the early stages of the Old West to the beginnings of the Industrial Age. His photographs, distributed across the nation and overseas, form a valuable record of life in the growing colonies of America's western frontier. He recorded poignant moments of everyday life among the Mormon pioneers, and documented events of national import. These images speak to us from the past, and convey a sense of both reality and nostalgia.

NOTES

1. For a complete genealogy of the Savage family, see appendix A.
2. Savage, "Life History," manuscript. Unless otherwise cited, all quotations in this chapter have been excerpted from this source.
3. *Deseret News,* June 6, 1925.
4. "Sister Clench," to Marianne Clark Sharp, 1966, regarding her grandfather, Henry Puzey. In Savage Book of Remembrance.
5. See letters in Savage Book of Remembrance.
6. Savage Journals, December 31, 1887.
7. Newsboys in nineteenth-century Salt Lake City, as elsewhere, were ususally fatherless children who were paid near-slave wages for their work. These boys were often the sole providers of income for their poor families, and worked in harsh conditions. For a complete discussion of the child labor reforms in Utah and the events that led to them, see Bradley.
8. *Deseret News,* July 23, 1936.
9. *Salt Lake Tribune,* October 17, 1895.
10. *Deseret News,* 1904, no exact date, copy in Savage Scrapbook.
11. *Deseret News,* July 19, 1881.
12. Savage, "Success or failure, Which?"; Savage, "What can a poor boy do to help himself?"
13. *Deseret News,* no date. Copy in Savage Scrapbook, with a note stating, "The last article written by Papa."
14. Copy of announcement in Savage Scrapbook.
15. Savage Journals, January 21, 1888.
16. Savage Journals, October 13, 1888.
17. Handwritten note on a picture in the Savage Book of Remembrance.
18. Garrick.
19. Savage Journals, May 4, 1892.
20. For a detailed account of the temple completion and the photographers who documented it, see Wadsworth's *Set in Stone, Fixed in Glass.*
21. Savage Journals, April 4, 1893.
22. Savage Journals, April 6, 1893.
23. Savage Journals, September 8, 1893.
24. Savage Journals, September 20, 1893.
25. Savage Journals, September 20, 1893.
26. Undated newspaper clipping in Savage Scrapbook.
27. Savage Journals, April 6, 1894.
28. Schofield.
29. Savage Journals, 1894 (undated).
30. Garrick.
31. Garrick.
32. Wadsworth, *Through Camera Eyes,* 155.
33. Savage Journals, June 4, 1899.
34. Annie Smith married John Calhoun Clowes on March 10, 1866; she married C. R. Savage on October 15, 1895.
35. Copy of advertising letter in Savage Scrapbook.
36. Savage Journals, January 6, 1909.
37. Romney, nibley and Taylor quotes from D. S. Spencer, in *The Salt Lake Daily Telegraph,* February 4, 1909.
38. Kenneth C. Kerr, in *The Salt Lake Daily Telegraph,* February 4, 1909.
39. Copy of newspaper clipping in Savage Scrapbook, source and date unknown.

AFTER the death of Charles Savage, the Art Bazar continued to be run by his three sons. Ralph still managed the photograph gallery, but was hampered by his progressive hearing loss. He was known as a good photographer in his own right, and many church and civic leaders had their portraits taken by him.

In 1911, the leaders of the Mormon Church were shocked to learn that Gisbert Bossard, an apostate member of the church, had smuggled a small detective camera into the Salt Lake Temple and photographed the interior. Although some photographs had been taken of the interior of the temple during construction, no pictures of the inside of the finished structure had ever been made for public display. The great reverence in which church members held the temple made any public exhibition of it offensive. When it became known that the pictures taken in the temple were to be sold to the highest bidder for eventual publication and ridicule, the Saints were outraged, and church leaders met to decide on a course of action. They decided that, rather than let the temple be disgraced by lurid tales told in a sensational manner, the church itself would publish a book showing the beautiful rooms of the temple. As a renowned photographer and faithful Latter-day Saint, Ralph Savage was chosen to photograph the temple rooms. This book, entitled *The House of The Lord*, explained in words and pictures the purpose and sacred nature of the temples of the Latter-day Saints Church. The accompanying text was written by noted Latter-day Saint scholar James E. Talmage. The public announcement by church leaders of this decision removed the aura of secrecy surrounding the unauthorized photographs, and rendered them worthless. No sale of the Bossard pictures ever took place, although they were displayed in a lantern-slide show in the East that closed after only a few days due to lack of interest.[1]

Several years after Savage's death, a devastating fire occurred at the Art Bazar, nearly repeating the destruction of the previous fire. It began in the warehouse located across the alley and behind the Art Bazar, which held the framing department, toy department, and photo gallery, as well as the stock of glass-plate negatives secured by Charles during his travels. The warehouse was connected to the main store on the second floor by a covered wooden bridge. In August of 1911, a plumber working under the building reportedly ignited the fire, destroying the entire building and its contents.[2] The main building of the Art Bazar was left intact, but the loss of inventory from the fire was a severe financial blow to the business. The glass-plate negatives, procured over the last twenty-five years of Savage's life, were lost. One report states that at least some of them may have been stored in the basement of the Savage home, but later were thrown out by family members when they cleaned the basement, as they were considered to be of no value.[3]

After the fire, the Savage family continued to run the Art Bazar, focusing mainly on the retail trade in artist's materials, novelties, toys, and picture frames. Photography gradually dwindled in importance, although the Art Bazar developed and finished Kodak film for amateur photographers throughout the inter-mountain

FIGURE 94.
Portrait of Charles R. Savage, c. 1902.
Collection of Harrison Brothers.

area. Despite Ralph Savage's photographic expertise, the business did not thrive as it had during Charles' lifetime. This was due in part to a lack of firm business leadership. George Savage, who had assumed management of the retail store, was reluctant to maintain large quantities of stock from the Kodak Company. The contract with Kodak specified that an adequate supply of products be stocked, however, and the Art Bazar consequently lost that contract and similar ones with other suppliers.[4]

As Savage's sons reached retirement age, members of the family lost interest in the business, and the Art Bazar closed its doors for good on December 31, 1926. The building on 12-14 Main Street was later used by several businesses, most recently by the Austin Art Studio and the Murdock Travel Agency. In the 1970s it was razed to make way for modern high-rise buildings.

Charles Savage's journals, scrapbook, and Book of Remembrance were passed down through the family to Mrs. Marianne Clark Sharp, daughter of Luacine Savage and J. Reuben Clark, Jr. In 1974, the journals and one of the scrapbooks were donated to the Harold B. Lee Library Archives at Brigham Young University in Provo, Utah. A copy of the other scrapbook, the Savage Book of Remembrance has recently been donated to the L.D.S. Historical Department Archives.[5] Many collections of Savage's photographs exist in museum archives across the country,[6] and help preserve the rich photographic record of the West created by Charles Roscoe Savage, pioneer photographer.

NOTES

1. For the complete history of this episode, see Wadsworth, *Set in Stone, Fixed in Glass*, epilogue.
2. Garrick.
3. Marianne Sharp Clark, as told to Nelson Wadsworth. (Personal communication, February 1992.)
4. Garrick.
5. The original is still in the possession of Mrs. Sally Sharp Lloyd, Salt Lake City, Utah.
6. For a listing of these collections, see Bibliography.

PLATES

Photographs by
Charles R. Savage

PLATE I.
C. R. Savage's photo wagon in the desert southwest, c. 1867. Stereoview, collection of Nelson Wadsworth.

PLATE 2.
Zion Canyon, Utah, c. 1870. Albumen print, collection of Nelson Wadsworth.

PLATE 3.
View of the Wasatch mountains, taken from Liberty Park in Salt Lake City, c. 1886. Albumen print, collection of the L.D.S. Historical Department.

PLATE 4.
Miner's shack in Park City, Utah, c. 1874. Cabinet card, collection of L.D.S. Historical Department.

PLATE 5.
Ogden City, Utah, viewed from the west, c. 1898. Albumen print, collection of the Utah State Historical Society.

PLATE 6.
Thistle, Spanish Fork Canyon, Utah, c. 1875. Mammoth plate for the Rio Grande Western Railway, collection of Carl Mautz.

PLATE 7.
View of Ontario Mine in present-day Park City, Utah, c. 1885. Albumen print, collection of the Utah State Historical Society.

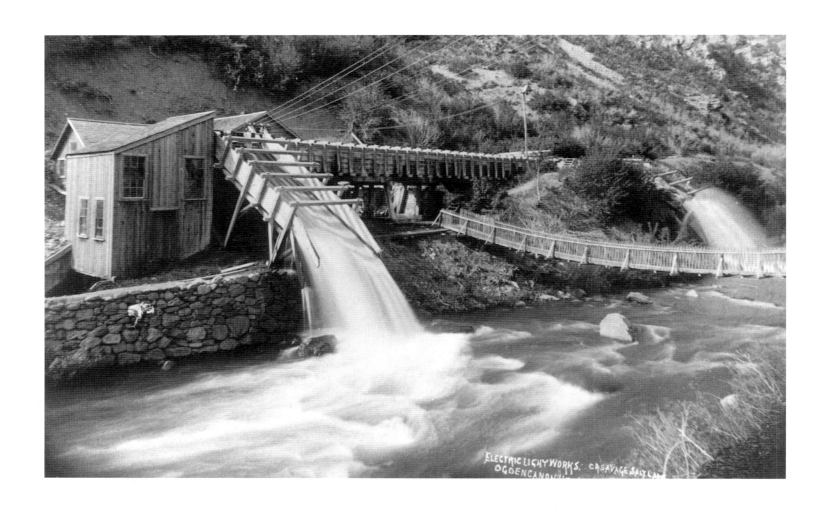

PLATE 8.
Electric Lights Works, Ogden Canyon, Utah. Collection of the Utah State Historical Society.

PLATE 9.
Great Shosone Falls, c. 1888. Albumen print, collection of Harrison Brothers.

PLATE 10.
Farm scene near Springville, Utah, c. 1876. Albumen print, collection of the Utah State Historical Society.

PLATE 11.
Lake Florence, Cottonwood Canyon, Utah, c. 1897. Note artist George Ottinger seated in the foreground with the easel. The other man is probably Alfred Lambourne.
Albumen print, collection of the Utah State Historical Society.

PLATE 12.

Unknown location, c. 1897. George Ottinger is crouched in the foreground and members of the Savage family are seen elsewhere in the picture. Cabinet card from the Savage Book of Remembrance.

PLATE 13.
Street scene in the mining town of Alta, Utah, c. 1885. Albumen print, collection of the Utah State Historical Society.

PLATE 14.

"The modern cliff-dwellers." Mining shacks are perched on a cliff above the Eagle River, Colorado, c. 1888. Albumen print, collection of Harrison Brothers.

PLATE 15.
Fort Douglas Band, Salt Lake City, Utah, c. 1870. Carte-de-visite, collection of L.D.S. Historical Department.

CARMEL MISSION NR MONTEREY. CAL.

PLATE 16.
Carmel Mission, near Monterey, California, during restoration, 1884. Cabinet card, collection of L.D.S. Historical Department.

PLATE 17.
Hotel Del Coronado, from the ocean, California, c. 1892. Albumen print, collection of L.D.S. Historical Department.

PLATE 18.
Bridal Veil Falls, Yosemite Valley, California, c. 1884. The notation "Instantaneous" in the title shows that this is one of Savage's early attempts to use the new dry or "instantaneous" photographic plates. Albumen print, collection of Don Parmiter.

PLATE 19.
Point Lobos, near Monterey, California, c. 1887. Albumen print, collection of Don Parmiter.

PLATE 20.
Logging at Lake Tahoe, California, c. 1890. Albumen print, collection of Utah State Historical Society.

PLATE 21.
Scene from the construction of the Salt Lake City Temple, c. 1877. Stereoview, collection of Bill Lee.

PLATE 22.
Cathedral Rocks, Yosemite, California, c. 1879. Cabinet card, collection of L.D.S. Historical Department.

PLATE 23.
Brigham Young University, Provo, Utah, c. 1900. University President Karl O. Maeser and L.D.S. Church President Joseph F. Smith and his buggy drawn by white horses.
Albumen print, collection of L.D.S. Historical Department.

PLATE 24.
Interior of Zion's Cooperative Mercantile Institution (Z.C.M.I.), Salt Lake City, Utah, c. 1878. Albumen print, collection of L.D.S. Historical Department.

UNVEILING THE STATUE
OF BRIGHAM YOUNG JULY 1897

PLATE 25.
Unveiling of the statue of Brigham Young, Salt Lake City, Utah, 1897. Albumen print, collection of L.D.S. Historical Department.

FIGURE 26.
Salt Lake Tabernacle under construction, c. 1865. Carte-de-visite, collection of Carl Mautz.

PLATE 27.
Workmen quarrying granite blocks for the Salt Lake Temple, at the mouth of Little Cottonwood Canyon,
c. 1874. Stereoview, collection of Bill Lee.

PLATE 28.
Salt Lake City Post Office, c. 1890. Albumen print, collection of L.D.S. Historical Department.

PLATE 29.
Z.C.M.I Building, Salt Lake City, Utah, c. 1899. Albumen print, collection of L.D.S. Historical Department.

PLATE 30.
Ute Indian family, c. 1870. Cabinet card, collection of Harrison Brothers.

PLATE 31.
Unidentified view of miners and equipment. Cabinet card, collection of Bill Lee.

PLATE 32.
Baptism of Shivwits Indians, near St. George, Utah, March, 1875. Stereoview, collection of L.D.S. Historical Department.

PLATE 33.
Joining of the rails celebration at Promontory, Utah, 1869. Stereoview, collection of Carl Mautz.

PLATE 34.
"Indian washerwomen, Tucson," stereoview from Views of the Great West, Arizona Series, *c. 1882. Collection of Jeremy Rowe.*

144

FIGURE 35.
"View on the Colorado—Yuma City Steamboat Landing, SPRR Bridge," stereoview *from* Views of the Great West, California Series, *c.1882. Collection of Jeremy Rowe.*

PLATE 36.
"Interior of moquis Village, South of the Colorado River, Moin Coppee," stereoview from Views of the Great West, California Series, *c. 1882. Collection of Jeremy Rowe.*

PLATE 37.
Ute Indian family, c. 1879. Cabinet card, collection of Harrison Brothers.

PLATE 38.
"Bannock Indians," stereoview from Views of the Great West, Utah Series, *c. 1882. Collection of Jeremy Rowe.*

PLATE 39.
Double exposure stereoview of Charles Savage and his friend, William Foster possibly taken by Ralph Savage, c. 1900. When viewed with a stereoviewer, the hats on the two men's heads seem to blink on and off. From Savage Book of Remembrance.

PLATE 40.
Portrait of Ethel Young. Albumen print, collection of the Utah State Historical Society.

PLATE 41.
Portrait of Lennie Louise Savage Riter, daughter of Charles Savage, in stage costume, c. 1900. Cabinet card, collection of the Utah State Historical Society.

PLATE 42.
Portrait of Ebenezer Beesley, cabinet card, collection of the Utah State Historical Society.

PLATE 43.
Portrait of Ray Savage, C. R. Savage's son, c. 1885. Cabinet card, collection of the Utah State Historical Society.

PLATE 44.
Studio portrait of Salt Lake City police officers Malin and Pyper, c. 1895. Cabinet card, collection of the Utah State Historical Society.

PLATE 45.
Studio portrait of unknown subjects. Albumen print, collection of the Utah State Historical Society.

PLATE 46.
Portrait of Orrin Porter Rockwell, famed bodyguard to Joseph Smith and Brigham Young, c. 1870.

FIGURE 47.
Stagecoach bound for Salt Lake City, Utah, c. 1880. Stereoview, collection of Joe Silva.

Savage Genealogy

THE Savage family originally came from northern England. During the War of the Roses a John Savage fought on the side of the Lancasters, and after their victory was rewarded for his service with knighthood and a Barony. The castle of Sir John Savage became known as Rock Savage. This was the source of the commonly used name Roscoe in the Savage family. (C.R. Savage's son Roscoe E. Savage was often called by his nickname, "Rock") After the days of Cromwell the Savage family lost the Barony, and eventually moved to southern England. Although family tradition ties Charles Savage to this ancient family, his direct line has been traced back only two generations, to the late 1700's. Further research on his genealogy is still being done by his descendants.

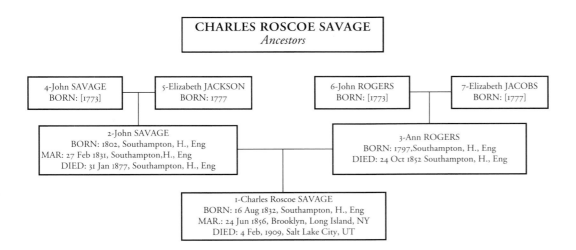

CHARLES ROSCOE SAVAGE
Ancestors

4-John SAVAGE
BORN: [1773]

5-Elizabeth JACKSON
BORN: 1777

6-John ROGERS
BORN: [1773]

7-Elizabeth JACOBS
BORN: [1777]

2-John SAVAGE
BORN: 1802, Southampton, H., Eng
MAR: 27 Feb 1831, Southampton,H., Eng
DIED: 31 Jan 1877, Southampton, H., Eng

3-Ann ROGERS
BORN: 1797,Southampton, H., Eng
DIED: 24 Oct 1852 Southampton, H., Eng

1-Charles Roscoe SAVAGE
BORN: 16 Aug 1832, Southampton, H., Eng
MAR.: 24 Jun 1856, Brooklyn, Long Island, NY
DIED: 4 Feb, 1909, Salt Lake City, UT

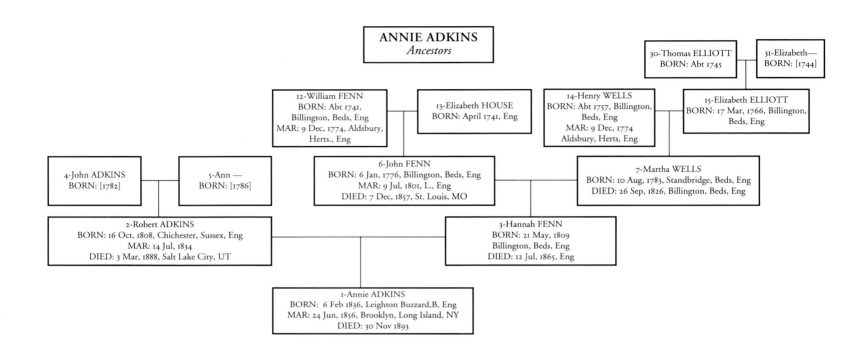

ANNIE ADKINS
Ancestors

30-Thomas ELLIOTT
BORN: Abt 1745

31-Elizabeth—
BORN: [1744]

12-William FENN
BORN: Abt 1741,
Billington, Beds, Eng
MAR: 9 Dec, 1774, Aldsbury,
Herts., Eng

13-Elizabeth HOUSE
BORN: April 1741, Eng

14-Henry WELLS
BORN: Abt 1757, Billington,
Beds, Eng
MAR: 9 Dec, 1774
Aldsbury, Herts, Eng

15-Elizabeth ELLIOTT
BORN: 17 Mar, 1766, Billington,
Beds, Eng

4-John ADKINS
BORN: [1782]

5-Ann —
BORN: [1786]

6-John FENN
BORN: 6 Jan, 1776, Billington, Beds, Eng
MAR: 9 Jul, 1801, L., Eng
DIED: 7 Dec, 1857, St. Louis, MO

7-Martha WELLS
BORN: 10 Aug, 1783, Standbridge, Beds, Eng
DIED: 26 Sep, 1826, Billington, Beds, Eng

2-Robert ADKINS
BORN: 16 Oct, 1808, Chichester, Sussex, Eng
MAR: 14 Jul, 1834
DIED: 3 Mar, 1888, Salt Lake City, UT

3-Hannah FENN
BORN: 21 May, 1809
Billington, Beds, Eng
DIED: 12 Jul, 1865, Eng

1-Annie ADKINS
BORN: 6 Feb 1836, Leighton Buzzard,B, Eng
MAR: 24 Jun, 1856, Brooklyn, Long Island, NY
DIED: 30 Nov 1893

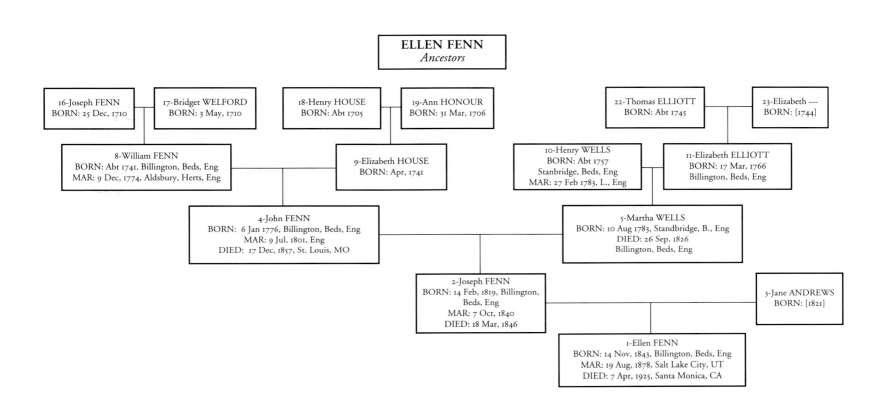

ELLEN FENN
Ancestors

16-Joseph FENN
BORN: 25 Dec, 1710

17-Bridget WELFORD
BORN: 3 May, 1710

18-Henry HOUSE
BORN: Abt 1705

19-Ann HONOUR
BORN: 31 Mar, 1706

22-Thomas ELLIOTT
BORN: Abt 1745

23-Elizabeth —
BORN: [1744]

8-William FENN
BORN: Abt 1741, Billington, Beds, Eng
MAR: 9 Dec, 1774, Aldsbury, Herts, Eng

9-Elizabeth HOUSE
BORN: Apr, 1741

10-Henry WELLS
BORN: Abt 1757
Stanbridge, Beds, Eng
MAR: 27 Feb 1783, L., Eng

11-Elizabeth ELLIOTT
BORN: 17 Mar, 1766
Billington, Beds, Eng

4-John FENN
BORN: 6 Jan 1776, Billington, Beds, Eng
MAR: 9 Jul, 1801, Eng
DIED: 17 Dec, 1857, St. Louis, MO

5-Martha WELLS
BORN: 10 Aug 1783, Standbridge, B., Eng
DIED: 26 Sep, 1826
Billington, Beds, Eng

2-Joseph FENN
BORN: 14 Feb, 1819, Billington,
Beds, Eng
MAR: 7 Oct, 1840
DIED: 18 Mar, 1846

3-Jane ANDREWS
BORN: [1821]

1-Ellen FENN
BORN: 14 Nov, 1843, Billington, Beds, Eng
MAR: 19 Aug, 1878, Salt Lake City, UT
DIED: 7 Apr, 1925, Santa Monica, CA

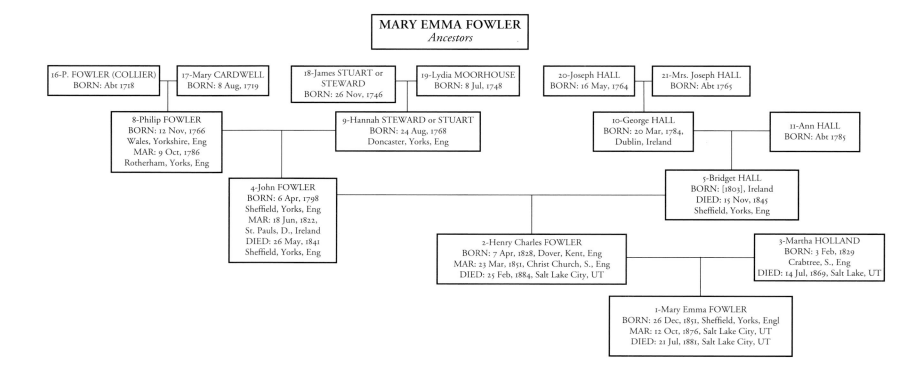

16-P. FOWLER (COLLIER)
BORN: Abt 1718

17-Mary CARDWELL
BORN: 8 Aug, 1719

18-James STUART or
STEWARD
BORN: 26 Nov, 1746

19-Lydia MOORHOUSE
BORN: 8 Jul, 1748

20-Joseph HALL
BORN: 16 May, 1764

21-Mrs. Joseph HALL
BORN: Abt 1765

8-Philip FOWLER
BORN: 12 Nov, 1766
Wales, Yorkshire, Eng
MAR: 9 Oct, 1786
Rotherham, Yorks, Eng

9-Hannah STEWARD or STUART
BORN: 24 Aug, 1768
Doncaster, Yorks, Eng

10-George HALL
BORN: 20 Mar, 1784,
Dublin, Ireland

11-Ann HALL
BORN: Abt 1785

4-John FOWLER
BORN: 6 Apr, 1798
Sheffield, Yorks, Eng
MAR: 18 Jun, 1822,
St. Pauls, D., Ireland
DIED: 26 May, 1841
Sheffield, Yorks, Eng

5-Bridget HALL
BORN: [1803], Ireland
DIED: 15 Nov, 1845
Sheffield, Yorks, Eng

2-Henry Charles FOWLER
BORN: 7 Apr, 1828, Dover, Kent, Eng
MAR: 23 Mar, 1851, Christ Church, S., Eng
DIED: 25 Feb, 1884, Salt Lake City, UT

3-Martha HOLLAND
BORN: 3 Feb, 1829
Crabtree, S., Eng
DIED: 14 Jul, 1869, Salt Lake, UT

1-Mary Emma FOWLER
BORN: 26 Dec, 1851, Sheffield, Yorks, Engl
MAR: 12 Oct, 1876, Salt Lake City, UT
DIED: 21 Jul, 1881, Salt Lake City, UT

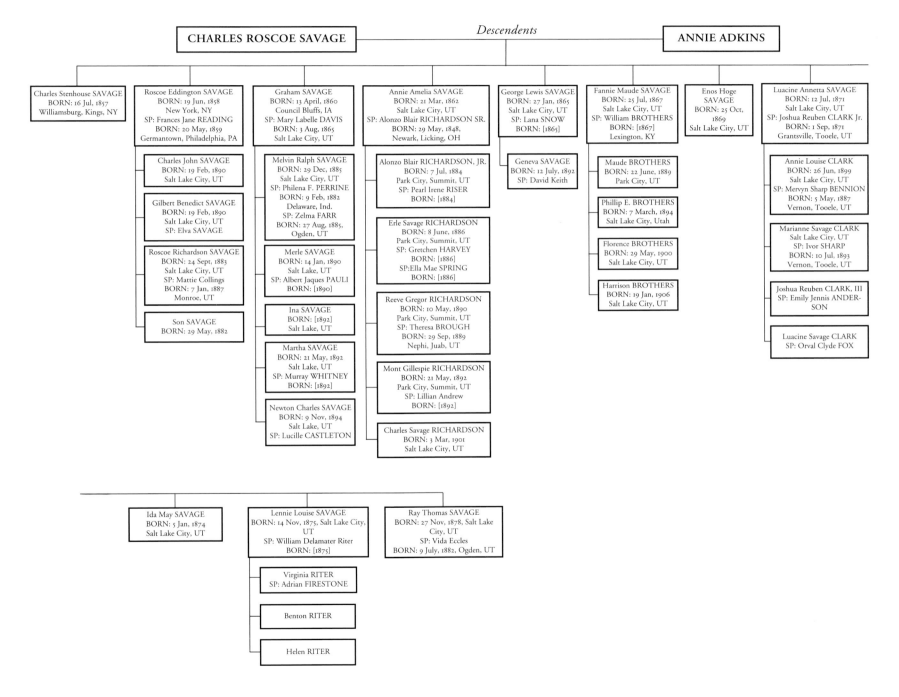

CHARLES ROSCOE SAVAGE — *Descendents* — ANNIE ADKINS

Charles Stenhouse SAVAGE
BORN: 16 Jul, 1857
Williamsburg, Kings, NY

Roscoe Eddington SAVAGE
BORN: 19 Jun, 1858
New York, NY
SP: Frances Jane READING
BORN: 20 May, 1859
Germantown, Philadelphia, PA

- **Charles John SAVAGE**
  BORN: 19 Feb, 1890
  Salt Lake City, UT

- **Gilbert Benedict SAVAGE**
  BORN: 19 Feb, 1890
  Salt Lake City, UT
  SP: Elva SAVAGE

- **Roscoe Richardson SAVAGE**
  BORN: 24 Sept, 1883
  Salt Lake City, UT
  SP: Mattie Collings
  BORN: 7 Jan, 1887
  Monroe, UT

- **Son SAVAGE**
  BORN: 29 May, 1882

Graham SAVAGE
BORN: 13 April, 1860
Council Bluffs, IA
SP: Mary Labelle DAVIS
BORN: 3 Aug, 1865
Salt Lake City, UT

- **Melvin Ralph SAVAGE**
  BORN: 29 Dec, 1885
  Salt Lake City, UT
  SP: Philena F. PERRINE
  BORN: 9 Feb, 1882
  Delaware, Ind.
  SP: Zelma FARR
  BORN: 27 Aug, 1885,
  Ogden, UT

- **Merle SAVAGE**
  BORN: 14 Jan, 1890
  Salt Lake, UT
  SP: Albert Jaques PAULI
  BORN: [1890]

- **Ina SAVAGE**
  BORN: [1892]
  Salt Lake, UT

- **Martha SAVAGE**
  BORN: 21 May, 1892
  Salt Lake, UT
  SP: Murray WHITNEY
  BORN: [1892]

- **Newton Charles SAVAGE**
  BORN: 9 Nov, 1894
  Salt Lake, UT
  SP: Lucille CASTLETON

Annie Amelia SAVAGE
BORN: 21 Mar, 1862
Salt Lake City, UT
SP: Alonzo Blair RICHARDSON SR.
BORN: 29 May, 1848,
Newark, Licking, OH

- **Alonzo Blair RICHARDSON, JR.**
  BORN: 7 Jul, 1884
  Park City, Summit, UT
  SP: Pearl Irene RISER
  BORN: [1884]

- **Erle Savage RICHARDSON**
  BORN: 8 June, 1886
  Park City, Summit, UT
  SP: Gretchen HARVEY
  BORN: [1886]
  SP: Ella Mae SPRING
  BORN: [1886]

- **Reeve Gregor RICHARDSON**
  BORN: 10 May, 1890
  Park City, Summit, UT
  SP: Theresa BROUGH
  BORN: 29 Sep, 1889
  Nephi, Juab, UT

- **Mont Gillespie RICHARDSON**
  BORN: 21 May, 1892
  Park City, Summit, UT
  SP: Lillian Andrew
  BORN: [1892]

- **Charles Savage RICHARDSON**
  BORN: 3 Mar, 1901
  Salt Lake City, UT

George Lewis SAVAGE
BORN: 27 Jan, 1865
Salt Lake City, UT
SP: Lana SNOW
BORN: [1865]

- **Geneva SAVAGE**
  BORN: 12 July, 1892
  SP: David Keith

Fannie Maude SAVAGE
BORN: 25 Jul, 1867
Salt Lake City, UT
SP: William BROTHERS
BORN: [1867]
Lexington, KY

- **Maude BROTHERS**
  BORN: 22 June, 1889
  Park City, UT

- **Phillip E. BROTHERS**
  BORN: 7 March, 1894
  Salt Lake City, Utah

- **Florence BROTHERS**
  BORN: 29 May, 1900
  Salt Lake City, UT

- **Harrison BROTHERS**
  BORN: 19 Jan, 1906
  Salt Lake City, UT

Enos Hoge SAVAGE
BORN: 25 Oct, 1869
Salt Lake City, UT

Luacine Annetta SAVAGE
BORN: 12 Jul, 1871
Salt Lake City, UT
SP: Joshua Reuben CLARK Jr.
BORN: 1 Sep, 1871
Grantsville, Tooele, UT

- **Annie Louise CLARK**
  BORN: 26 Jun, 1899
  Salt Lake City, UT
  SP: Mervyn Sharp BENNION
  BORN: 5 May, 1887
  Vernon, Tooele, UT

- **Marianne Savage CLARK**
  Salt Lake City, UT
  SP: Ivor SHARP
  BORN: 10 Jul, 1893
  Vernon, Tooele, UT

- **Joshua Reuben CLARK, III**
  SP: Emily Jennis ANDER-
  SON

- **Luacine Savage CLARK**
  SP: Orval Clyde FOX

Ida May SAVAGE
BORN: 5 Jan, 1874
Salt Lake City, UT

Lennie Louise SAVAGE
BORN: 14 Nov, 1875, Salt Lake City,
UT
SP: William Delamater Riter
BORN: [1875]

- **Virginia RITER**
  SP: Adrian FIRESTONE

- **Benton RITER**

- **Helen RITER**

Ray Thomas SAVAGE
BORN: 27 Nov, 1878, Salt Lake
City, UT
SP: Vida Eccles
BORN: 9 July, 1882, Ogden, UT

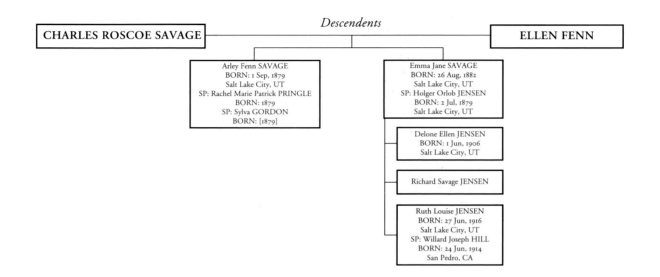

C. R. Savage Photographic Trips

Dated information in quotation marks are direct quotes from Savage's journals. All other information is obtained from Savage Journals under the dates shown unless otherwise noted.

1861

June 7-Aug. 29: Trip across plains to Utah, some pictures possibly taken of Chimney Rock and Devil's Gate, among others.

June 9: Salt Lake Daily Telegraph, Panorama of city (Salt Lake City).

1866

This is the year of the "Photographic Tour" across the plains. No journal entries on photos taken. The only partial list of photos taken is in the article: Savage, Charles R., "A Photographic Tour of 9000 Miles," *The Philadelphia Photographer*, Jan. 1867, 287-9, 313-6. and in two related news items. One is in the *Philadelphia Photographer*, Jan. 1867, 32; the other is the *Deseret News*, Aug. 30, 1867. The partial list of photos includes "A Mormon camp, preparing to start across the plains," "A camp of immigrants at Wyoming" [Nebraska] (may be the same photo), "A home in Nebraska," "O'Fallon's Bluff, S. Platte," "Farm Scene on Steven's Creek, Nebraska," "Devil's Gate," "Sweetwater," "Castle Rock, N. Platte," and pictures of Fort Kearny and Chimney Rock.

Feb. 22: *Salt Lake Daily Telegraph*. View of temple block.

1867

Dec. 5: *Salt Lake Daily Telegraph*. Recent trip to Shoshone Falls, Bear River hotel.

1868

June 5: *Salt Lake Daily Telegraph*. Savage and Ottinger, City of Rocks and Snake River.

Aug 27: *Salt Lake Daily Telegraph*. Trip to Montana and Idaho.

Oct. 29: *Salt Lake Daily Telegraph*. Savage and Ottinger. Small article in advertisement section, where Ottinger

describes the progress being made on the UPRR tunnels and grades by Mormon work teams. Also a description of the "fine bridge at Devil's Gate," etc. Mentions Savage's pictures of railroad workers, pictures of tunnel construction in Weber Canyon, etc.

1869

April 21: "Letters from two or three individuals . . . having seen our picture in *Harper's Weekly* of the Great Shoshone Falls"

April 23: "Took two stereoscopes from top of Kimball and Lawrence building."

April 27: "Took negative of Townsend house."

May 8-10: Promontory, driving of golden spike.

May 22: "Visited Geological camp on the Bench. Saw Mr. Sullivan, the photographer of the outfit."

May 25: "Picture of endowment house."

May 30: "Started this morning for the Devils Gate where I succeeded in taking some fine negatives. I spent the day in hard work, having taken 13 stereoscopic and 2 4x4 negatives in the 2 days during the trip." Pictures mentioned of Echo Canyon, Echo City, Devil's Gate, 1000 Mile Tree, Weber Canyon, Tunnel #3, Brigham Young's residence.

June 9: *Salt Lake Daily Telegraph*, p. 209. Notice of Promontory pictures for sale.

June 10-16: "Started for Big Cottonwood canon with Geological Expedition in charge of Mr. [Timothy O']Sullivan." Pictures of Paradise Valley, Cottonwood Lake.

July 10-15: Fort Bridger, Church Buttes, Uinta Mountains, Smith's Fork.

Sept. 23-30: Green River, Pyramid and Tea-Pot Rocks, Palisades, rocks at Green River, Burning Rock, Sherman, Cheyenne.

1870

Mon., Jan. 10: Driving of the final spike of the Utah Central Railroad.

Tues., Jan. 18: "Started to Ogden by UCRR."

Fri., Feb. 26: "Left Salt Lake City for Dixie at 10 A.M." This is the trip to Southern Utah taken with Brigham

Young's company. Photographs mentioned include: Cottonwood Creek, Black Mountain, St. George, St. Thomas, Piede Indians, "a group of the persons visiting the Colorado" [Brigham Young's entourage], Black Canyon of the Colorado, fort at St. Thomas, Joshua Cactus, North Fork of the Virgin River, Springdale, Zion's Canyon (16 views), Rockville, Virgin City, Tocquerville, Cedar City, and the meeting house at Beaver.

Wed., April 20: "Points for Views Elco, first point thence to Carlin, several views on the road, the Humboldt Narrows, machine shop, etc. at Carlin, stopped at Palisade, Groups of miners with ore. Palisade rocks, odd scenes."

Fri., May 13: California—Sacramento, including picture of "Engine House and engines," Winnamucca, Palisades, Rocklin, Sacramento, Bloome Cut, Clipper ship, Cape Horn, Blue Canyon, and Truckee.

Thurs., June 9-14: California (same trip?) "Stayed at Alta all night, went with section hands up to ½ way point, took 3 fine views north fork, Rock cut," view of hydraulic washing at Gold Run, Dutch Flat, Gold Run, Secret Town trestle, Mary's Lake, "Scene near the Station," Summit, Donnor Lake.

Sat., Aug. 6: "Send samples of Bear River Petroleum Works . . ."

Sun., Aug. 7-16: Snow sheds at Aspen, Bridger, Uintas, Bridger Hotel, Church Buttes Station, picture of Judge Carter's family, Green River, Fort Steele, Tunnel #1, and Mr. Stockwell's house.

1871

Jan. 4: *Salt Lake Herald*, article, "Mr. C. R. Savage has furnished us with a number of very beautiful stereoscopes and other views of Southern Utah, the Union Pacific and Central Pacific railroads and other points."

May 5: Salt Lake Herald, advertisement, "The Lightning View Wagon will soon visit the CANONS of Utah. Those wishing views or SKETCHES of MINES, CLAIMES, [sic] &c. will please leave their orders with C. R. Savage at the Pioneer Art Gallery."

May 28-June 1: California, including Colfax and picture of someone's home, cafe at Colfax, Bloomer Cut.

June 8: *Salt Lake Herald*, "Our old friends C. R. Savage and G. M. Ottinger Esq. are "doing" the choice spots of the Sierras, photographing and sketching all the weird beauties of Cape Horn . . . with a hand-rail car to pass up and down the road . . . met at Alta last Sunday where they were taking their usual Sabbath rest . . .

Aug. 8: *Salt Lake Herald*, article which states: Mr. C. R. Savage has secured a number of beautiful views of the finest scenery of American Fork Canon, which combines some of the most picturesque and enduring scenes to be found in the country. Mr. Savage started this morning for Little Cottonwood . . . . Also an advertisement: "Just published–Magnificent views on AMERICAN FORK & LITTLE COTTONWOOD CANONS taken by C. R. Savage and for sale at the Pioneer Art Gallery. Come and see them."

Aug. 13: *Salt Lake Herald*, article which consists of a tribute to C. R. Savage as a photographer. Contains an expanded version of the remarks in the Aug. 8th article. Also mentions views available from American Fork and other canyons, Montana, Idaho, the Colorado River and surrounding desert country, Southern Utah, Northern Arizona, and the Sierras, including Cape Horn. Also states that Savage views are for sale in New York, London, Edinburgh, and Paris.

1873

Wed., March 26: "Working at the Germania Separatory Works. Took 5 or 6 fine negatives."

Sat., May 3: "Took some fine negatives of the city [Salt Lake City] from residence of Mr. Backin."

1874

Tues., June 9: "Send . . . 1 each of Cliff House, unmounted."

Thurs., July 2: "Went up to Bingham Canyon to photograph the Revere Mine from the top of the Nez Perce Hill. Fine view of the Wahsatch Range."

Tues., July 21-Aug 3: Colorado . . . Green River, Colorado Springs, Garden of the Gods, Cheyenne Canyon, Grand Canyon, and Monument Park.

Fri., Oct. 16-18: Omaha.

Fri., Oct. 30-Nov. 1: Elkhorn, Fremont, "in company with J. R. S. Cobb."

1875

Thurs., March 4-23: "Fred Lambourne and self leave Salt Lake City for Dixie today." Virgin River, Rockville, Little Zion Valley, Virgin City, desert, St. George, Paragonah, baptism [of Shebit Indians]

May 22: *Frank Leslie's Illustrated Newspaper* 40:1025, 169, 171 Article and lithograph reproduction of Savage picture of Indian baptism.

Mon., June 21: "Left SL City for Cal today in company with R. F. Gesler."

Wed., July 28-30: "Ralph and I leave for the West today."

Fri., July 30: "Mr. Oaks Humboldt 2 geyser pic Yellowstone Park."

Oct. 23: *Frank Leslie's Illustrated Newspaper* 41:1047, 101, 103. Illustrated with Savage photo of "Needle Palm, or Yucca Brevifolia.-.Also Specimens of the Barrel Cactus (Cereus Le Contei) Found in the Deserts of Arizona."

1876

Centennial World's Fair, Philadelphia. There is no list of photos taken, but Savage apparently took many photos of the fair, since he later made a lantern slide show of the fair and showed it throughout the Salt Lake area. Savage was in Philadelphia for the fair from Jan. 1-31.

Fri., Oct. 22-24: "Left Platte Valley in company of Fred Lambourne." Columbus, Schell Creek.

1877

Jan. 22-23: "Left Salt Lake City for Bingham Canon to photograph the old Telegraph Mining Co. Works . . . taking views of the gulch, works, railroad, and other objects connected with the old Telegraph Mining Co. Took snow pictures, 15 seconds with smallest stop, success."

May 19: Ontario Silver Works in Parly's Park.

May 28: "Went up to the Falls of Provo River, named them Silver Thread Falls—took views of them."

June 5-10: "Started for California in company with Fred Lambourne." Tahoe, Emerald Bay.

Sept. 4: "Started for California in company with Doc. D. E. Benedict. Visited Nevada—Virgin City and other places. Nothing of note appeared during the trip."

1878

March 5-17: "Off for California with Ralph." "Fort Yuma, desert, Old San Bernardino, orange groves …"

May 28: "Took views of the St. George Temple."

Aug. 31: "In company with F. Lambourne visited Alta, . . . Took views of Lake Minnie, head of Little Cottonwood."

Oct. 27-Nov. 11: "Left for New York in company with Doc. Benedict." Chicago.

Dec. 10: "At San Francisco with Brother Dunbar, good time."

1878-79

Small notebook, not a regular journal. Notes about a trip west, including a trip into the desert. These entries are all in pencil and are very difficult to read. Total in notebook on trip west – about 2 pages.

1879

April 19: "Roscoe and self leave for a trip to Yuma and Maricopa Wells and Arizona via the CPRR."

May 16: "George and self left for Snake River via the UTN railway. Got a fine view of the new railway bridge."

May 31-June 4: "Roscoe and myself start for the Yosemite Valley today . . . Decide to go to Virginia City as we cannot go to the Yosemite."

July 1: "Rock and self safe and sound in the Yosemite Valley, viewing with good luck thus far, wonderful place, surpassing anything I ever saw."

Aug. 5-Oct. 15: Savage on trip to England with G. M. Ottinger, mainly seeing the sights and speaking in branches of the Church. No mention of anything photographic.

1880

March 13-April 4: "Left for California in company with F. Lambourne." Sulano at Benion, desert, Old Yuma, San Xavier, Tuscon, Maricopa, Pinio village, "cactus studies."

1881

May 2: "Started for California and Arizona with Bro. Sanborne . . . Next day. . . started for Monterey . . . Went to [Lurdeburge ?] in New Mexico."

June 11: "Ralph and I leave for San Francisco tonight."

Sept. 10: "George and I go to Butte Montana on a trip taking views." Snake River.

Nov. 3: "I start for Boston on the 4th in company with Fred Lambourne . . . return home on the 26th."

1882

Jan. 17-29: "Sister Savage and self leave for San Francisco."

Sacramento. April 21-May 16: "Ralph and I leave on the 22nd for California." "3 doz. wanted of Mariposa Grove with Tunnel in tree." "Ralph and I go to the Mojave Desert to get Cactus views. We also photograph the new depot of the CPRR." Cape Horn and Long Ravine.

Oct. 20-Nov. 5: "Will Young, son of Hans Young, with self start for the east today, stopping at Omaha." *Harper's Weekly,* unknown date, lithograph print from a Savage picture of the Utah Commission. (Utah commission originally organized in 1882.) There is a second Savage journal for 1882 that mentions the Utah Commission. This is apparently a notebook in which he was taking notes of the proceedings of the Utah Commision, talking about the crowds there, and what was done. About 3 or 4 pages total. There is no mention of taking a photo of the Commission at that time.

1883

March 16-24: "Ralph and self go to San Francisco today."

1884

Jan. 1:"Out with the Tabernacle Choir, took a view of the entire party . . ."

Jan. 19-26: "Leave for Chicago today . . . in company with Rob Matson and wife from the UP."

Mar. 24: "Viewing east part of city."

April 29: "Took some new negatives of the city today."

April 30: "More new views today."

May 5: "Got views of Camp Douglas."

May 6-17: "Start for Frisco with Fred Lambourne on CPRR." Palisades, Golden Gate Park and Cliff House, Monterey, Hotel El Monte in Monterey, Cyprus Point, Signal Rock, and Carmel Mission.

May 24-June 6: "Off for the Union Pacific in Chicago." "Need to get some views of Omaha, but it was cloudy, and a storm was brewing so gave up the idea and moved west to Sherman." Views of Sherman, Plum Pudding Rocks near Sherman, Dale Creek, view of station.

June 17-18: "Bro Maeser and I got to Park City." "Work around the Ontario." [Ontario Silver Mine]

June 20: "Send pic of Devils Gate to Mr. Fitzpatrick, Evanston."

June 25-July 4: "Bro Maeser and I start for San Francisco." "Took views of Humboldt." "Took photo of the Boca brewery on the Truckee line."

Aug. 26-Sept. 5: "George, Fred Lambourne and I start for the Yellowstone Park today, via the N & N." "Left for the upper geyser basin and commenced work. Take 14 negatives. The eruptions of the geysers very grand." "Worked on the geysers." "Start for the Yellowstone Falls . . . Took 22 negs by the dry process." "Took 3 large 18 x 22 negatives of Falls and Canon." "Went to Yellowstone lake."

Oct 23: "Help with George in and around Park City and Echo."

Oct. 30-Nov. 21: "Leave for the east via the D&RG alone." "Took 20 negatives today in and around the Black and Cimmeron Canons." Needles, Cimmaron Canyon, Menshall Pass, Denver, Omaha. "Go to Philadelphia today, and visit Mrs. Ottinger." New York, Chicago, Canada.

1885

Feb. 28-March 12: "John Reading and self go to San Francisco."

April 18: "Go back to Provo and take a few views."

May 1: "Viewing in Provo."

May 11-12: "Go to Logan to photograph the Temple. George goes with me."

May 14-31: "Start for Chicago in company with George . . ." Rock Springs. "At Cheyenne on our way home, and get successful views of Cheyenne and Dale Creek."

Oct 13-16: "George Ottinger and myself start for the states today, and stop overnight at Green River." "Walk out and take some large views around the rocks at Green River." "We visit Boston, Chicago and New York."

1886

May 24-April 5: "Leave with F. Lambourne for San Francisco, CA." "Work instantaneous plates at the Cliff House." Delta, Mt. Shasta.

May 9: "At Fort Herriman with Bro Mull."

May 19: "Joseph Simmons and myself leave for Denver via the D&RG, viewing, stop off at Mill Fork … Take picture around the Red Narrows, but with indifferent results."

1887

March 26: "Off for California Fred + I."

May 30: "Went to the Pen with the Tab Choir … Took views of the inside and exterior."

June 17: "I make some views in the Utah Pen."

Aug. 4: "Photograph the Manti Temple today."

Aug. 24: "Photograph the Crescent RR, and get views of Park City."

1888

April 24: "Fred Lambourne and self take a trip into the Columbia River, and have a fine time getting some good views."

May 17: "Wells goes with me on a trip to Denver, returning via the Union Pacific. He is a very agreeable companion and get some fine views."

May 30: "Take views at Provo Canon Falls today. Bro Smoot furnishes team."

June 9: "I make a fine selection of views on the Columbia River in company with Fred Lambourne."

Aug. 30: "Take photos of the rowing match at Lake Point today."

Oct. 13: Nov. 6 "I start for the states today via the UP and Burlingham to Chicago"

1889

April 5: "During the last 2 weeks in company with Alfred Lambourne I visit lower California, Santa Barbara, Santa Cruz, big trees and cumulus where is laid the stones written in Mrs. Jacksons [sic] Am successful and return home the first morning of Conference."

May 3-5: "Go to Castle Gate and Green River to make views."

May 29: "In company with Dr. Jos. Benedict I visit the Yosemite Valley and make 98 negatives."

July 11: "Go with Bro Evan Stevens out to Sherman on the UP Ry for a few days."

July 24: "I went to Salt Lake to make some photography."

Sept. 3: "We leave today by the Rio Grande Western for an artistic trip on the line of the new wide gauge of the D&RG. A car is furnished to me by Mr. Bennet, magnate. Lucy, Fan, Ray, Rock, and Fred Lambourne go with us. During our trip on the car we visit many of the most noted points on the D&RG. Our wives, Mama and the girls enjoyed the trip immensely. We are treated with the greatest courtesy by the officials of the D&RG Ry."

1890

March 10-22: "In company with Bro John Hafen I leave for the coast to get snow pictures of Cape Horn." Truckee, summit, Colfax, Cape Horn, San Francisco.

April 22: "Am busy catching views of different points during the fine weather."

Oct. 11: "I go to San Francisco in company with my son-in-law, H. B. Richardson. On the way I am troubled with an attack of opthalmogia, which affects my sight for the balance of the year. Visit Montana and take some views."

1891

March 8: "Went out with H. M. Stanley and friends to Salt Lake."

May 9-21: "Leave for San Francisco to [illegible] C.W. Penrose." Shasta Springs, Mt Shasta, Santa City.

June 15: "Get some fine views from San Francisco."

June 23-25: "Ralph and I go to Summit on a viewing trip." Summit, Soda Springs.

Aug. 20: "We go to Soda Springs due to photograph the Blackfoot cattle ranch."

Sept. 4: "Roscoe and self leave on Friday for a viewing trip up Brian Canon on Sat 3rd . . ."

Sept. 7: "Return home from Logan. Some good negatives."

Sept. 17-22: "John Hafen and self start out on the RGW. Stop at Thistle." Shale Grand River, "Summit of the Midland."

Oct. 13: "Took views in the Spanish Fork Canon of the Sugar House."

Oct. 31-Nov. 8: "Ray and self leave for California tonight." "Photographing around San Fran."

1892

March 9: "Out with M. Bennet Gettes and Ray Goy . . . Taking views on the loop on the Tintic Branch RG DRy."

March 19-31: "Off for California with Bro Talmage." San Francisco. "Off for the Salinas Valley to Santa Margarita." "Go back to San Miguel and take pictures of the old Mission founded in 1798. I took Bro Talmage in the robes of a priest in the corridor. Return back to El Paso de Robos, the oak Pass." Monterey, San Jose. "Go to San Fran and visit the opium dens and purlieus of China town."

April 4: "The conference which began on the 3rd and closed with the placing of the capstone on the temple was one of the best of any one that I have attended . . ." "Photographs taken of this event."

June 15: "During the month of June I visit Lake Tahoe and Cal, with John Hafen."

July 21-Aug. 1: "Today I leave for the Teton Range in Idaho on the east of the Teton Basin . . . I am accompanied by Sis. Clowes and Bro. Eddington." Rexburg, Teton Basin, falls of Teton Peaks, Teton Lakes, Trail Creek Canon, Jackson's Hole and the Snake River country, Fish Creek, Lake Creek, Mt. Merrin, Mary Moore Landing, Blue Grass Creek.

Sept. 3-19: "Start with George to the east tonight, via the RGW taking through car to Chicago." Columbian Fairgrounds, New York, Boston.

1893

Feb. 12-16: "Leave this forenoon for California with my outfit, accompanied by Will Ottinger." San Francisco "Return home after making some successful views."

March 10: "During the most of this week I have been taking views of School houses in Tooele Co. – in Company with Bro Robinson School Supt with whom I have an agreeable time."

April 4: "Take a picture of the special window in the Sealing room to day – and see the Temple most beautiful in Every detail."

Sat., April 8-14: "I go to Chicago this morning to arrange for my exhibit at the Worlds Fair."

May 14-24: "Leave for San Fran and the coast in company with Bro. [John] Reading." Fowle's Station. "Go out on the Sugar Pine R.R., 22 miles to make some views." San Francisco. "Make some views in the building devoted to the floral show." Monterey, Menlo Park.

June 8-12: "Leave in little car furnished by the R.G.W. for the taking of some nice views on the road. Bro

Eddington, John Hafen, and Arley [Savage] – go with me – take some fine views at Thistle." "Visit Salina."

June 14-16: "At Thistle again . . ." "Stop at Nolan switch to hunt some new views in Price Canon." "Go on to Green River."

Sept. 15-26: "To night George and self start for the World's Fair via the U.P. Ry." Chicago, St. Louis.

Nov. 15: "I go over to California to see if work is to be done at the Midwinter Fair and have a pleasant time visiting Mr. Todd . . ." Undated article, unknown Salt Lake newspaper, about Savage's trip to the East, including comments on the Chicago World's Fair. Copy in Savage Scrapbook.

1894

Early 1894: Trip with Brother Dunbar "to see whales."

April 11-23: "Rock and I go west to California . . . Take some views of Golden Gate Park."

May 18: "Went to Scofield to take the views of the coal mines . . . Splendid views of fine coal owned in the R.G.W. and U.P. Rys."

June 17: "During the last 2 weeks in company with Charlie Rogers I have visited Bear Lake, Brigham, and Wells in trying to get a selection of good views."

June 21: "Start westward with S. K. Gillespie for Lake Tahoe . . . Secure a good number of views and leave for San Francisco on the 26th."

1895

June 22: *Deseret News.* Letter to the editor regarding a trip along the Rio Grande Southern lines and Silverton Railroads in southern Colorado, also another article in the same paper referring to this same letter to the editor.

1900

Oct. 13: *Deseret Evening News.* Report of trip to Island Park on Henry's Fork of Snake River. Savage went in a private railroad car to photograph this area. (Oregon Short Line RR.)

Savage Items in Institutional Collections

ARCHIVE	NUMBER	COMMENTS
Amon Carter Museum 3501 Camp Bowie Blvd. Fort Worth, TX 76107-2695 (817) 738-1933	17 items: 12 views, 5 stereos	Salt Lake City, etc., c. 1870-1880. 1 Indian picture, 7 views in album of W. H. Jackson images.
Arizona Historical Society 949 E. Second St. Tucson, AZ 85719 (602) 628-5775	6 items: varied sizes	Indian family, portrait of Brigham Young, 2 portraits of Savage, etc.
Boston Public Library P.O. Box 286 Boston, MA 02117 (617) 536-5400	57 items: 53 stereos, 4 views	Utah scenes, Central Pacific and Union Pacific views, etc.
California Historical Society 2090 Jackson St. San Francisco, CA 94190 (415) 567-1848	5 items	
California Museum of Photography University of California Riverside Riverside, CA 92521 (714) 787-4787	3 items: 2 stereos 1 view	2 views of Salt Lake City, 1 of American Fork Railroad.
California State Railroad Museum Library 111 I St. Sacramento, CA 95814 (916) 323-8073	6 items: all stereos	All from Union Pacific series, taken in Weber and Echo Canyons, also Green River.
Church of Jesus Christ of Latter-day Saints Historical Dept. Archives Salt Lake City, UT 84150 (801) 240-2272	300-500 items	Landscapes and city scenes, mainly of Utah and surrounding areas. Few portraits, some of Indians.
Cline Library Northern Arizona University P.O. Box 6022 Flagstaff, AZ 86001-6022 (602) 523-2171	1 Item: stereo	Mouth of the Black Canyon of the Colorado River.
Colorado Historical Society 1300 Broadway Denver, CO 80203-2137 (303) 866-3682	25 items: 12 stereos, 13 views	Railroad, Salt Lake City, Indians, landscape views.

ARCHIVE	NUMBER	COMMENTS
George Eastman House 900 East Ave. Rochester, NY 14607-3970 (716) 271-3361	153 items: 132 stereos, city scenes, etc. 5 cdv 15 other	Landscape views, Indians, Salt Lake.
Harold B. Lee Library Brigham Young University Provo, UT 84602 (801) 378-4170	approx. 600 items: partially catalogued cdv, cabinet, stereo and large views	Mostly landscapes and city scenes, some portraits.
Idaho Museum of Natural History Idaho State University Campus Box 8096 Pocatello, ID 83209-0009	1 item	Ute Indian family.
J. Paul Getty Museum 401 Wilshire Blvd. Santa Monica, CA 90401 (301) 458-9811	130 items: 116 stereos 12 prints 2 books	Railroad, Indians, Salt Lake City, Echo Canyon, etc.
Library of Congress Prints and Photographs Washington, D.C. 20540 (202) 707-5000	more than 30 items, many stereos	Idaho, Utah and Montana views, Indians, etc.
Library Photo Archives University of Kentucky Lexington, KY 40506 (606) 258-8634	3 items	
Museum of New Mexico 113 Lincoln Ave Santa Fe, NM 87503 (505) 827-2559	15 items	
National Museum of American History Smithsonian Institution Washington, D.C. 20560 (202) 357-2700	approx. 30 items	Utah scenes, Central Pacific and Union Pacific railroads, some portraits.
National Museum of Natural History Smithsonian Institution Washington, D.C. 20560 (202) 357-4560	approx. 60 items	Mainly Indian portraits and groups.
Nebraska State Historical Society P.O. Box 82554 Lincoln, NB 68501 (402) 471-4754	4 items: 2 cartes-de-visite	Mormon pioneers in Nebraska, Indian portrait, bridge.

ARCHIVE	NUMBER	COMMENTS
Nevada Historical Society 1650 N. Virginia St. Reno, NV 89503 (702) 688-1190	1 item	Portrait.
New Orleans Museum of Art P.O. Box 19123 City Park New Orleans, LA 70179 (504) 488-2631	1 item: view	Emerald Bay, Lake Tahoe, California.
New York Public Library 5th Ave. & 42nd St. New York, NY 10018-2788	135 items: many stereos, scenes, etc.	Utah, Nevada, Colorado, railroad.
Oregon Historical Society 1200 S.W. Park Avenue Portland, OR 97205-2483 (503) 222-1741	24 items: 4 stereos, 19 views, 1 portrait.	Columbia River Gorge, Salt Lake City, Brigham Young, etc.
Park City Historical Society P.O. Box 555 Park City, UT 84060 (801) 645-5135	3 items: single views	Park City and local mines.
San Diego Historical Society P.O. Box 81825 San Diego, CA 92138 (619) 232-6203	1 Item	Copy negative of cdv. Portrait of Zina Huntington, mother of Wm. D. Huntington.
Seattle Art Museum Seattle Center Seattle, WA 98112 (206) 447-4710	3 items	
Stanford University Museum of Art Stanford, CA 94305-5060 (415) 723-4177	150 items in single leather album	Title of album: "San Francisco Before and after the Earthquake of 1906."
The Art Museum McCormick Hall Princeton University Princeton, NJ 08540	15 items	
The Huntington Library 1151 Oxford Rd. San Marino, CA 91108 (818) 405-2179	122 items: 63 stereos 40 views 9 books	Stereos are mainly railroad-related. views and cdvs are of Salt Lake City and area

ARCHIVE	NUMBER	COMMENTS
The Newark Public Library 5 Washington St. Newark, NJ 07101-0630 (201) 733-7828	11 items: all carte-de-visite views	Views of buildings and streets in Salt Lake City, c.1870s-80s.
Union Pacific Railroad Museum 1416 Dodge St. Omaha, NB 68179 (402) 271-3305	75 items	Union Pacific Railroad related photographs.
Union Station Museum 25th & Wall Ave. Ogden, UT 84401 (801) 629-8444	75-100 items	Many copy photos, few originals. Mainly of railroad or Ogden area.
University of Nevada, Reno Reno, NV (702) 784-1110	10-20 items, mostly stereos	Nevada, Great Basin, incl. Lake Tahoe, mining scenes, etc.
Utah State Historical Society 300 W. Rio Grande Salt Lake City, UT 84101 (801) 533-5755	approx. 225 items mostly catalogued	Also 400-500 glass plate negatives from the Savage studio from 1919-1929; portraits.
Washington State Historical Society 315 N. Stadium Way Tacoma, WA 98403	1 item	Portrait of Brigham Young.
Wyoming State Museum 2301 Central Avenue Cheyenne, WY 82001 (307) 777-7031	19 items: all stereos	Utah views, circus elephant, etc.
Yale University Art Gallery Dept. of Prints, etc. 2006 Yale Station New Haven, CT 06520 (203) 432-4055	1 item	Lion House, Salt Lake City, Utah.
Yosemite National Park Museum P.O. Box 577 Yosemite National Park, CA 95389 (209) 372-0281	12 items: 10 cabinets 1 mammoth size view 1 stereo	Yosemite.

Duplicate biographical sketches or articles about Savage containing no original material have been omitted. Also, a number of newspaper references that contain duplicate material, especially photographic advertisements, have been omitted in the interest of space. Many Savage pictures were used as illustrations in newspaper articles, etc., even years after his death, and these, too, have been omitted.

Andrews, Ralph W. *Picture Gallery Pioneers.* New York: Bonanza Books, 1964, 152-68.

Arrington, Leonard J. *Great Basin Kingdom: An economic history of the Latter-day Saints.* Lincoln: University of Nebraska Press, 1966.

"Back from the East: C. R. Savage Tells About His Travels Since Leaving Salt Lake," newspaper article about Savage's trip to the World's Fair in Chicago, and visits to Boston and New York (1893). Exact date and newspaper unknown. Copy in Savage Scrapbook.

Benion, Louise Clark. "My recollections of my grandfather, C. R. Savage," August 1992. Unpublished MS in author's possession, taken from an interview with Mrs. Benion.

Best, Gerald M. *Iron Horses to Promontory.* San Marino: Golden West Books, 1964.

Bissell, Hezekiah. "Recollections." MS, Cheyenne: Wyoming State Archives and Historical Department.

Bradley, Martha S. "Protect the Children: Child Labor in Utah, 1880-1920." *Utah Historical Quarterly* 59:1 (Winter 1991), 52-71.

Brey, William. *John Carbutt on the frontiers of photography.* Cherry Hill, New Jersey: Willowdale Press, 1984.

"Brigham Young - Brigham Young's Residence." *The Illustrated London News* 39:117 (November 16, 1861), 502.

Brothers, Harrison. "Recollections of my Grandfather, C. R. Savage." July 28, 1992, unpublished MS in author's possession.

Browne, C. F. *The Complete Works of Artemus Ward.* New York, 1898, rev. ed.

Bullington, Neal R., "Timpanagos: The National Parks Mini-cave," *Stereo World* 4, no. 5 (Nov.-Dec., 1977), 6-7

Carter, Charles W. Negative Collection, L.D.S. Church Historical Department Archives, Salt Lake City, Utah.

Carter, John E. "Photographing across the Plains: Charles R. Savage in 1866." *Nebraska History* 71:2 (Summer 1990), 58-63.

Carter, Kate B. "Early Pioneer Photographers." *Our Pioneer Heritage,* vol. 18. Salt Lake City: Daughters of Utah Pioneers, 1975, 249-301.

—. *Heart Throbs of the West,* vol. 5. Salt Lake City: Daughters of the Utah Pioneers, 1944, 46-61.

—. *Heart Throbs of the West,* vol. 9. Salt Lake City: Daughters of the Utah Pioneers, 1948, 107-10, 130, 133, 134, 140, 149, 426.

—. *Heart Throbs of the West,* vol. 12. Salt Lake City: Daughters of the Utah Pioneers, 1955, 425.

—. "Journal of Rachel Emma Wooley Simmons." *Heart Throbs of the West,* vol. 11. Salt Lake City: Daughters of the Utah Pioneers, 1950, p. 185.

—. "The McCune Family." *Our Pioneer Heritage,* vol. 1. Salt Lake City: Daughters of the Utah Pioneers, 1975, 313-6.

The City of the Saints in Picture and Story. Salt Lake City: Deseret News Press, 1906.

Clark, Luacine A. Savage. *Life Sketch of Charles Roscoe Savage.* Unpublished MS, copy in Savage Book of Remembrance.

—. *Life Sketch of Annie Adkins Savage.* Unpublished MS, copy in Savage Book of Remembrance.

Clayson, Ruby Thornton Brown. *Biography of Edward Covington.* Unpublished MS in Harold B. Lee Library Film Collection (call no. 920 #52). Brigham Young University, Provo, Utah..

Clayton, William, to George Q. Cannon. July 16, 1861, in the *Millennial Star,* xxxiii (1861), 506.

Crofutt, George A. "Crofutt's New Overland Tourist and Pacific Coast Guide . . ." vol. 1. Chicago: The Overland Publishing Co., 1879. 322 pages, and "over 100 beautiful engravings . . . the photographs were by Savage, of Salt Lake City, and Watkins and Houseworth, of San Francisco."

Deseret Evening News. October 27, 1877. "Juvenile Representations." Notice that Savage's photo montage, "Utah's Best Crop," is for sale at the gallery.

—. October 17, 1895. Advertisement for Democratic election ticket, with Savage listed as candidate for state senator.

—. January 14, 1898. "Microscopical Society. Interesting lectures delivered by Mr. C. R. Savage . . . on Life in Artic Seas . . ."

—. January 22, 1916. "Veteran Artist still busy with palette and brush." Article about the life of George Ottinger.

—. July 8, 1916. "'Charlie' Savage in 1856." Copy of early daguerreotype picture of Savage.

Deseret News, October 10, 1860. Advertisement.

—. February 18, 1863. Advertisement, "Ambrotype apparatus for sale."

—. October 14, 1863. Advertisement, "Good Photographic Printer Wanted."

—. December 9, 1863. Advertisement, "Opening of new gallery 1st door south of the Council House."

—. March 29, 1866. Notice of "Fine Pictures" taken by Savage and Ottinger's.

—. July 5, 1866. Notice that Savage was "on his way from the East."

—. August 30, 1866. Notice of Savage's return from the east after his photographic tour.

—. October 6, 1875. "The New Art Gallery."

—. September 12, 1877. Notice of portrait of Brigham Young for sale at the gallery.

—. June 27, 1883. "A destructive fire."

—. July 23, 1936. Notice of unveiling of C. R. Savage monument and drinking fountain in Salt Lake City.

Deseret News Weekly. July 30, 1862. Advertisement for straw hats made by Mrs. C. R. Savage.

—. October 29, 1862. Advertisement for Savage and Ottinger gallery, lists types of pictures made.

—. July 5, 1866. Notice that Savage was "on his way from the East" on his photographic tour.

—. September 26, 1866. Advertisement, "Photograph-ic and Artist's materials."

Fleming, Paula Richardson, and Judith Laskey. *The North American Indian in early pictures.* New York: Dorset Press, 1988.

Fowler, Don D. *Photographed all the Best Scenery, Jack Hiller's Diary of the Powell Expeditions, 1871-1875.* Salt Lake City: University of Utah Press, 1972.

Fowler Family Papers. Collection of Regional History, Cornell University Library, Ithaca, New York.

Frank Leslie's Illustrated Newspaper. "The Snow Blockade" 34:861 (March 30, 1872), 45. One sketch and two photographs by Savage used as illustrations.

—. "Southern Utah - Baptism of Qui-Tuss, Chief of the Shebit Tribe of Indians, Together with One Hundred and Thirty of the Same Tribe, at St. George" 40:1025 (May 22, 1875), 169, 171. Article and lithograph reproduction of Savage picture.

—. "Needle Palm, or Yucca Brevifolia - Also Specimens of the Barrel Cactus (Cereus Le Contei) Found in the Deserts of Arizona" 41:1047 (October 23, 1875), 101, 103. Illustrated with Savage photo.

Garrick, John A. "My recollections of C.R. Savage." November 1983. Inglewood, California. Unpublished MS, copy at L.D.S. Church Archives, Historical Department, Salt Lake City.

Harper's Weekly. "City and Valley of the Great Salt Lake" (August 18, 1866). Article containing lithographs taken from Savage photos, possibly written by Savage.

—. "The Niagara of the West - Great Shoshone Falls - Photographed by Savage and Ottinger, Salt Lake City" 13:642 (April 17, 1869), 244, 248. One illustration.

—. "The Overland Pony Express" 11:566 (November 2, 1867), 693-4. Six illustrations from Savage and Ottinger, including Ute and Snake Indians, and a copy of a painting by George Ottinger.

—. "Completion of the Pacific Railroad - Meeting of Locomotives of the Union Pacific and Central Pacific Lines: The Engineers Shake Hands - Photographed by Savage and Ottinger, Salt Lake City" 13:649 (June 5, 1869), 356.

—. Lithograph pictures of an overland Pony Express station at Cheese Creek and Chimney Rock from photographs by C. R. Savage. Also a lithograph of a Pony Express rider taken from a painting by

George Ottinger (November 2, 1867).

Heinerman, Joseph. "The Old Folks Day: A Unique Utah Tradition." *Utah Historical Quarterly* 53:2 (Spring 1985), 157-169.

History of Charles Savage. Six handwritten pages, unknown author, original written into Savage Book of Remembrance.

Hulmston, John K. "Mormon Immigration in the 1860's: The Story of the Church Trains." *Utah Historical Quarterly* 58:1 (Winter 1990), 32-48.

Humphrey's Journal of Photography and the Allied Arts and Sciences. March 15, 1864, 343. Letter to editor regarding plain paper photographs.

—. June 1, 1864, 45. Letter to editor about lime and gold toning bath.

—. January 15, 1865, 286-7. Praise for card pictures sent in by Savage.

—. March 15, 1865, 351-2. Letter to editor with comments about plateholders.

—. July 15, 1865, 95. Letter to editor with a new formula for collodion.

—. December 1, 1865, 239. Mention of a panoramic view of Salt Lake City.

—. March 15, 1867, 351-2. Article praising Savage photographs.

Hunter, Milton R. "Old Folks Day." *Beneath Ben Lomond's Peak, A History of Weber County, 1824-1900.* Salt Lake City: Deseret News Press, 1944, 146-52.

Huntington, Collis P., Papers. Stanford University Archives, Stanford, California.

Jackson, William Henry. *Time Exposure; The Autobiography of William Henry Jackson.* New York: Cooper Square Publishers, Inc., 1970.

Jensen, Andrew. *History of the Scandinavian Mission.* Salt Lake City: Deseret News Press, 1927, 106-7.

—. *Latter-day Saint Biographical Encyclopedia.* Salt Lake City: Andrew Jensen History Co., 1920, vol. 2, 620; vol. 3, 160; vol. 4, 384.

Jensen, Emma Jane Savage. *Life History of Charles R. Savage.* Unpublished MS, copies in Daughters of Utah Pioneer Museum Archives, Salt Lake City, and on microfilm at L.D.S. Historical Department, Salt Lake City.

Leslie, Mrs. Frank. *California, A Pleasure Trip from Gotham to the Golden Gate.* New York: G. W. Car-

leton and Co., Publishers, 1877.

Pattison, William D. "The Pacific Railroad Revisited." *Geographical Review,* January 1962, 25.

Philadelphia Photographer 2:21 (September 1865), 154. "Editor's Table." Two views of Salt Lake City by Savage mentioned.

—. 2:24 (December 1865), 207. "Editor's Table." Panoramic view of Salt Lake City by Savage received.

—. 3:26 (February 1866), 67. "Mormon views and portraits from Savage and Ottinger, Salt Lake City," includes panorama of Salt Lake City.

—. 3:30 (June 1866), 191. Notice that Savage was coming East to secure supplies, and having a wagon built to carry them home in.

—. January 1867, 32. "Editor's Table." Note that Savage had arrived home safely in Salt Lake City.

—. November 1867, 352. Letter to editor contesting views published on "redevelopment."

—. 13:154 (October 1876), 320. "A series of magnificent views on the Pacific Railroad."

—. 15:176 (August 1878), 255. Letter to editor from Savage describing new collodion formula.

Photographic Times 18:373, November 9, 1888, 540. Note that Savage is publishing *The Busy Bee.*

—. 21:514 (July 24, 1891), 365 and frontispiece. Two illustrations of Henry M. Stanley and his wife, taken by Savage as the explorer was on his way across the American continent.

—. December 25, 1891, 668. Article quoting a recent C. R. Savage article in the *Juvenile Instructor,* "How to be successful as a Photographer."

—. 24:650 (March 2, 1894), 143. Article describing Savage's attempts at "nocturnal photography" by burning celluloid rather than magnesium.

Pratt, George B. *Ogden City, Utah. Picturesque and Descriptive,* Neenah, Wisconsin: Art Publishing Company, 1889. Hardbound, many illustrations, some taken by Savage. Good example of Savage photographs used without his permission or credit.

Reeves, Brian D. *Hoary-Headed Saints.* Masters thesis, 1987. Department of History, Brigham Young University, Provo, Utah.

Reynolds, George, to George F. Gibbs, June 4, 1868, in the *Millennial Star,* xxx (1868), 443.

Richards, Bradley W. "Charles R. Savage, the Other

Promontory Photographer." *Utah Historical Quarterly,* vol. 60 (Spring 1992), 137-57.

Roberts, B. H. *Comprehensive History of the Church of Jesus Christ of LAtter-day Saints.* 6 vols. Salt Lake City, Deseret Books, 1930, 5:355.

Sabin, Edwin L. *Building the Pacific Railway, the Construction Story of America's First Iron Thoroughfare.* Philadelphia: J. B. Lippincott Co., 1919.

Salt Lake Daily Telegraph. May 28, 1865. Panoramic view of Salt Lake City given to Napoleon III.

—. December 13, 1867. Article about new frontage for gallery.

—. February 4, 1909. Obituary of Savage.

Salt Lake Herald. January 4, 1871. "Views of Southern Utah, the UPRR, and CPRR," etc.

—. May 5, 1871. "The Lightning View Wagon."

—. June 8, 1871. "Our old friends C. R. Savage and G.M. Ottinger Esq. are doing the choice spots of . . ."

—. August 8, 1871. "Splendid new book of views of SLC just received . . ."

—. August 13, 1871. Article stating that Savage pictures are for sale at his gallery.

—. September 13, 1871. Article stating that Savage pictures are for sale in New York, London, Edinburgh, and Paris.

Salt Lake Tribune. October 17, 1895.

—. February 5, 1901. "Our Art Gallery." Cartoon and paragraph lampooning Savage and his friend Alfred Lambourne.

Savage Book of Remembrance. Original in possession of Sally Sharp Lloyd, Salt Lake City. A scrapbook-type album containing articles, pictures, memorabilia and documents from Savage's life. A copy of this album is now held at the L.D.S. Church Archives.

Savage, Charles R. "About Choirs: The value of music in our assemblies." Article, date, and newspaper unknown, copy in Savage Scrapbook.

—. *Art Bazar Almanac.* Salt Lake City: Deseret News Co., 1883. One-page advertisement for the Art Bazar. Copy in L.D.S. Church Historical Department Archives, Salt Lake City.

—. *The Busy Bee.* A four-page newsletter and advertising paper published by Savage for several years beginning in 1883. Copies of some issues available at L.D.S. Historical Department, Salt Lake City, and in the Savage Scrapbook.

—. "The Coming Election: A Voice of Warning From the Man in the Moon." *Deseret News,* October-November 1904. Letter to the editor re Savage's views on local politics.

—. "Going the West for the Picturesque." Article describing railroad trip to British Columbia, Puget Sound, Oregon, and California, date and newspaper unknown, copy in Savage Scrapbook.

—. "How Can a Poor Girl Help Herself?" *Juvenile Instructor* 38:7 (April 1, 1903), 197-200.

—. *In and around Salt Lake City.* Denver: Frank S. Thayer, c. 1900. Large pictorial book, several editions available, one in possession of author, another in L.D.S. Historical Department Archives, Salt Lake City.

—. "The Lewis and Clark Expedition." Undated talk in Savage's handwriting, unpublished MS, copy in Savage Scrapbook.

—. "Life History." Autobiographical sketch of early life of Savage. Copy in Savage Book of Remembrance.

—. "Life on Other Worlds." Rough draft of talk written in Savage's handwriting, copy in Savage Scrapbook.

—. "No Church Interference." *Salt Lake Tribune,* October 1895. Letter to editor regarding Savage's candidacy for the Utah State Legislature.

—. "An Ocean Voyage on a Sailing Ship: Crossing the ocean in the Fifties with a company of Immigrants." Talk written for a youth group, unpublished MS in Savage's handwriting, copy in Savage Scrapbook.

—. "Our Home Products; Necessity of Sustaining Utah Industries." *Salt Lake Herald,* undated. Letter to editor, copy in Savage Scrapbook.

—. "A Photographic Tour of nearly 9000 miles." *The Philadelphia Photographer* 4:45 (September 1867), 287-9, 313-6.

—. "Plea of C. R. Savage for the saloon victims." *Deseret News,* date unknown. Letter to editor; handwritten note on article, "The last article written by Papa." Copy in Savage Scrapbook.

—. *Pictorial Reflex of Salt Lake City and vicinity, with condensed epitome of Utah's people, resources, climate and other information useful to visitors and residents.* Salt Lake City, 1894. Several editions ranging from

1893-1901 available in L.D.S. Historical Department, Salt Lake City.

—. "Red Letter Days!" Unknown date (c. 1896) or newspaper. Letter to editor regarding Old Folks Day.

—. *Sad Keels Profetic [sic] messenger for 1882 and Art Bazar Almanac.* Salt Lake City: Deseret News Co. 1882. One-page advertisement.

—. *Salt Lake City, and the way thither.* London, Edinburgh and New York: T. Nelson and Sons, c. 1870-3. Pictorial guide book, illustrated with twelve lithographs from Savage photos. Copies of several editions in the L.D.S. Church Historical Department Archives, Salt Lake City.

—. *Salt Lake City and Vicinity.* Salt Lake City, 1895. Album of views, published in several editions.

—. *Salt Lake City with a sketch of the route of the Central Pacific Railroad, from Omaha to Salt Lake City, and thence to San Francisco.* London, Edinburgh and New York: T. Nelson and Sons, 1871. Pictorial guide book, illustrated with twelve lithographs from Savage photos. Copies of several editions in the L.D.S. Church Historical Department Archives, Salt Lake City.

—. "A Sportsman's Paradise." *Deseret Evening News,* October 1900. Article about trip to Island Park on Henry's Fork of Snake River.

—. "Success or Failure, Which?" *Juvenile Instructor* 7:18 (September 15, 1902), 568-70.

—. "To the Pirates of Utah (Not of Penzance)." *Deseret News,* July 19, 1881.

—. "A Trip South with President Young in 1870." *Improvement Era* 3:4 (February 1900), 293-9; 3:5 (March 1900), 363-9; and 3:6 (April, 1900), 431-6.

—. "Trip to Salmon City, Idaho." October 14, 1897. Letter to editor in unknown newspaper. Copy in Savage Scrapbook.

—. "Under the Snow." Article in Boise City, Idaho, newspaper; a copy of article in *Salt Lake Herald* about a trip through Nevada during the winter. Undated copy in Savage Scrapbook.

—. "The Use of the Eyes." *Juvenile Instructor* 39:3 (February 1, 1904), 78-79.

—. *Views of Utah and Tourist's guide Containing a Description of the Views and General Information for the Traveller, Resident and Public General.* Salt Lake City, Utah, 1887, 30 pages, 16 pictures.

—. "What can a poor boy do to help himself?" *Juvenile Instructor* 38:1 (January 1, 1903), 1-5.

—. "With the Picturesque. The Crags and Peaks of Southern Colorado." *Deseret News,* June 22, 1895. Letter to the editor.

Savage, Charles R., and M. Virginia Donaghe. *Picturesque Utah; Albertype illustrations from original photographs by Chas R. Savage.* Denver: Frank S. Thayer Co., 1888.

Savage Family Album. In possession of Sally Sharp Lloyd, Salt Lake City, Utah. This album contains family portraits and group pictures of the Savage family.

Savage Journals, 1855-1909. Harold B. Lee Library Archives, Brigham Young University, Provo, Utah.

Savage Journal, 1881. Complete microfilm copy in the L.D.S. Church Historical Department Archives, in the Emma Jane Savage Jensen collection. Location of the original journal unknown.

Savage Missionary Journal, 1853. Original journal contained in the Savage Book of Remembrance. Copy in the L.D.S. Church Archives

Savage, Ralph. *A Brief Genealogy of C. R. Savage.* Unpublished MS, copy in Savage Book of Remembrance.

Savage Scrapbook. Harold B. Lee Library, Brigham Young University, Provo, Utah. Scrapbook of newspaper articles, advertising flyers, and announcements collected by Savage and his family.

Schofield, N. Y. "Charles R. Savage. A Phrenograph From a Personal Examination." *Salt Lake Herald,* April 18, 1887.

—. "Charles R. Savage, a Phrenograph from a Personal Examination." *The Character Builder* 5:3 (July 1904), 72-5.

Sharp, Marianne Clark. *Life of Annie Adkins Savage.* Unpublished MS, copy in Savage Book of Remembrance.

Slaughter, William W. "C. R. Savage: Pioneer legacy in black and white." *Pioneer* 41:5 (September-October 1994), 8-15.

Slaughter, William W., and W. Randall Dixon. "Utah under glass: An introduction to four prominent pioneer photographers of 19th-century Utah." *Sunstone* 2:2 (Summer 1977), 28-39.

Stern, Madeline B. "A Rocky Mountain Book Store: Savage and Ottinger of Utah." *Brigham Young University Studies* 9:1 (Autumn 1968), 144-54. Article on relationship between Savage and the phrenological firm of Fowler and Wells in New York.

Swackhamer, Barry A. "J. B. Silvis, the Union Pacific's nomadic photographer." *Journal of the West* XXXIII :2 (April 1994), 52-61.

Taft, Robert. *Photography and the American Scene*, 1938.

"The Mormons and their Religion." *Century Magazine (Scribner's Monthly)* 3:4 (February 1872), 396-408. Uncredited photos, evidence suggests that these were Savage photographs.

"The New Mormon Temple." *Illustrated American* 11:119 (May 28, 1892), 66-7. Two illustrations from Savage pictures.

Tullidge, Edward W. *History of Salt Lake City*. Salt Lake City: Star Printing Company, 1886.

Wadsworth, Nelson. *Set in Stone, Fixed in Glass: The great Mormon temple and its photographers*. Salt Lake City: Signature Books, Inc., 1992.

—. *Through Camera Eyes*. Provo, Utah: Brigham Young University Press, 1975.

—. "Zion's Cameramen: Early Photographers of Utah and the Mormons." *Utah Historical Quarterly,* vol. 40, 1972, 24-54. Preliminary version of *Through Camera Eyes.*

Wells, Samuel R. "Rocky Mountain Bookstore." *The American Phrenological Journal.* 47:5 (May 1868).

—. *The Illustrated Annuals of Phrenology and Physiognomy, for the years 1865-72.* New York: Samuel R. Wells, Publisher, 1872,

Whitney, Orson F. *History of Utah*. Salt Lake City: George Q. Cannon and Sons Co., 1893, 524-30.

Willumsen, Glen G. "Alfred Hart: Photographer of the Central Pacific Railroad," *History of Photography* 12:1 (January-March 1988), 63.

"Wonders of the Mighty Deep, C. R. Savage's interesting paper before Microscopical Society." Unknown newspaper and date, circa 1898. Copy in Savage Scrapbook.

INDEX